The Badge
Thoughts From A State Trooper

The Badge
Thoughts From A State Trooper

Jim Geeting

McKenna Publishing Group
Indian Wells, California

The Badge
Thoughts From a State Trooper

Copyright © 2003 by Jim Geeting

All rights reserved. No part of this book may be used or reproduced in any manner without written permission of McKenna Publishing Group, except in the case of brief quotations employed in reviews and similar critical works.

ISBN: 1-932172-09-2
LCCN: 2002117407

Cover design by Leslie Parker
Cover photo of Trooper Jim Geeting's badge by Cody Geeting

Visit us on the Web at: www.insomniac.com/mckenna

First Edition
10 9 8 7 6 5 4 3 2 1

Contents

Acknowledgments..9

Prologue..13

Chapter One:
About Cops...15

Chapter Two:
The Cop's World..45

Chapter Three:
Cops and Kids...77

Chapter Four:
Random Thoughts and Daydreams..........................101

Chapter Five:
End of Watch...125

About the Author...131

To my beautiful wife, Janet.
You took a cop's hardened heart
And softened it with beauty and laughter and passion.
You made my life mean something very good.
You made every dream come true.
You are my best friend. You are my smile. You are my life.

I love you.

And to my sons Cody and Cameron.
You took a cop's blackened soul
And taught it the joy of wrestling, giggles and unconditional love.
Of camp outs, good jokes and the wonder in a bug or a rock.
Of the hero I could be—simply by being a good dad.
I dreamed of you both, long before God sent you …

I love you too!

Acknowledgments

Thank you ...

This is the page every writer wants to write. The page where he thanks all of the people who made his first book possible. This is my turn. I am certain I will forget someone. I am already sorry.

The very first people who ever noticed I could lay down some words were my parents. I can remember writing a paper on America in the third grade and my Mom and Dad suggesting writing as a career choice. Of course, like most kids I ignored them. Then I became a cop. Now, at the age of forty-six, I have met my calling and have two decades of catching crooks, writing tickets and wearing a uniform. As usual, Warren and Shirley Geeting were right. I thank God every day they were my parents.

My Dad was a cop in Los Angeles and often wondered why, after seeing *his* career culminate in utter disgust at having to salute criminals before arresting them, his youngest son would follow suit. I don't know Dad, but the finest man I ever knew was a cop. Perhaps that is why.

My Mom worked in the medical profession as long as I remember, and taught my brother and me to laugh at life, at ourselves and to take pleasure in the wondrous joy in living. I love you guys and hope you are proud of me.

My brother Doug is a world famous and celebrity bush pilot, musician and author living in Talkeetna, Alaska. For forty-six years he has been the object of my envy, admiration and pride. I don't think I have ever said that until this moment. Don't fly too high, Doug! Thanks for the lifetime of examples you set for me.

My Field Training Officer, Trooper Ricky Dye has earned a place here as well. I reference him and his influence upon me several times in my writing, and am honored to have his friendship—even though he spilled his chew juice in my patrol car twice while training me. He once hid my patrol car when I left the keys in it (and unlocked) at the county jail, teaching me a valuable lesson on avoiding embarrassing letters to the Chief:

"Dear Colonel, the reason I lost my patrol car is..."

He laughed at me too many times to count but also taught me many skills and subtle tactics; all of which have kept me safe, alive and without bullet holes many times over my career. He wasn't smooth, but gruff, unpleasant and in my face when it came to my safety. He has survived several shootings as a trooper and has been highly decorated for his skill and valor. I will respect and admire him as long as I live and I thank God he is my friend.

Another trooper I want you to know about is Tom Adams. Thomas E. Adams of Lander—a fellow hardcore Republican who makes me look like a liberal. Gruff like Rick, Tommy has been my friend at times I deserved no friends. He cared enough about me to once call me "half-assed" and a "jerk" to my face in one sitting! Pardon my French, but Tom is blessed with a no nonsense "get to the point" attitude and one never needs an interpreter to figure out what Tommy really means. This is why you gotta love this guy. Tom, as the Wyoming Highway Patrol Association President, is the main reason Wyoming State Troopers today enjoy top pay and a good retirement plan. I will never let anyone forget that.

Holly Jackman is the publisher of the *Rock Springs Daily Rocket*

Miner, one of Wyoming's largest newspapers. She is an outstanding journalist, a veteran reporter and the reason my column, *The Badge*, was permitted to see print. She listened to my idea for a weekly column written by a plain-spoken, folksy but wordy cop. In it the discussion would be of the dynamic interaction between cops and the public, and the sometimes emotional world of law enforcement. There had been several months of bad press about "wrong cops," a group I discuss and I felt it was time to remind the public of the half-million of us doing it right. She agreed, and this book is the result. After two years of local exposure, we have collected the works and put them all in one place. Thanks, Holly! For your faith and patience on those missed deadlines, and your support—albeit always objective—of the good guys.

Finally, to the tens of thousands of my readers from whom email, letters and in person encouragement kept the dream alive, provided ideas for more material, and more than anything else proved I was right. You agreed the time had come for such a weekly chat between the cops and the public and I hope we addressed a few points of contention.

The work goes on. Every other week in the *Miner*, monthly in the *Casper Star-Tribune* and *Cheyenne Tribune-Eagle*, thousands of readers get a dose of me—a working cop who wants you to know that we're all in this together. Without cops, your world would be rough and out of control. Without you, a supportive and informed public, the job of the professional peace officer would be completely impossible. Like it or not we need each other.

I thank you all. For buying this book and for reading my column.

Trooper Jim Geeting
Wyoming Highway Patrol

Prologue

In the United States there are 750,000 men and women who will proudly give up their last breath and lay it all down to see you safely through. They are of every jurisdiction and level but all are sworn to protect you. They claim no superior instincts than you, but do their best to perform their task as though possessed with superhero virtues. Each day you get up, go about your day and then later go to bed feeling safe and secure, one, or several of them did their job. You are well and safe one more day. They are out there right now as you read this, giving you freedom to enjoy your life. Each and all are worthy of your honor and trust and are some of the very best of humanity.

Like everybody else, peace officers have regular lives with bills and car repairs, but then when it's time to go to work, their job is like no other. A career few can do, fewer *want* to do and even fewer survive. Their task? Simply to protect you—in a perfect, resolute way, without waiver, without glory, without compromise. And without mistakes. You expect that of them. It is an impossible edict but they try. All too often the decisions you debate and casually study over coffee were thrust upon them with milliseconds to act. And act they must, as indecision is *fatal* to a cop. Absolutely deadly.

The fact is you will probably never even meet in an official way unless circumstances invite them into your life. You can rest assured they might say something politically "incorrect" or perhaps even have bad breath, but you know what? Your life *will* be protected—your family *will* be safe—even if that cop must give up his life to achieve it. That's what *I'm* talkin' about! I'm talkin' about raw courage. I'm talkin' about shining service in the face of very vicious and sadistic bad guys.

Folks, each and every day the men and women I am so very proud to be associated with are concerned not about the 95% of you, but are interested and precisely focused on the other 5%. Those among us who would selfishly take, hurt and kill with no regard but for themselves. Those who do all they can to fill your kid's veins with dope, hurt you, steal from you, and destroy what you hold priceless. Among the many tasks you ask of your peace officers is the noble effort to stop those people. I say there is nothing more gallant than that effort. You have no better friend on this earth.

Chapter One
About Cops

The Truth

Some of my regular readers have been asking me to address a few of the most enduring myths about police work. Tell us the "real story" they say. While I am no authority on every cop everywhere in every circumstance, I have seen the real side to many of the mystical beliefs out there and can share my own experience with you. Please understand there are more than 750,000 cops in the United States and I only know a handful. But that handful is from north and south, both coasts and everywhere in-between. So here we go ... the myths and the truth.

Police work is glamorous. Yeah? Ever had a drunk hurl in your lap? How about down your defroster ducts? Ever been beaten to a pulp by the very woman you thought you were defending, suddenly deciding she loves her abusive husband after all as you try to arrest him?

Want more glamour? Handle human tissue and internal organs tossed all over the roadway in a crash. Or perhaps you'll find glamour when you are called to investigate a densely foul odor coming from an old, unvented apartment where a quiet, older citizen has lived for many years but no one has seen around for a few weeks. Yeah, baby! Hollywood has nothin' on this.

Cops get free stuff. Well, if this one's true somebody's gettin' mine! Other than the occasional cup of coffee or soda which, as I have written of before, is more a traditional gesture of respect than a payoff, I've always had to pay for my stuff. I am willing to learn, however, if someone is out there giving stuff away! Email me!

Cops just hang with other cops. While this one can be true in some places, it's not so much the rule. This is due in part, I think, to the small communities and close knit neighborhoods. People here in Wyoming don't care so much WHAT you do, only that you DO work hard if you can. My friends include mechanics, firefighters, writers, schoolteachers, energy workers, and miners and yes—a few really demented cops.

A badge is a free pass for traffic tickets. Well, this one depends a little bit on what the meaning of "is" is. If the meaning of "is" is "guarantees," then this is wrong. The world is full of cops who've been hammered by one of their own. If the meaning of "is" is "can be," then this is correct. While many cops do tend to let the minor stuff slide if they see "tin," just as many get red hot at a badge being shoved in their face as though it represents automatic immunity. In fact, this move has resulted in cops citing other cops when the original intent was only a warning. Personally, I'm afraid I'd be too embarrassed I screwed up to identify myself this way.

Police work is the most dangerous job on earth. Absolutely not. When it comes to occupational danger the stats say police work is way, way down the list. Know what's first? Underground mining. These people—and many in Wyoming who do this for a living—must be absolutely fearless and have incredible calm. Convenience store clerks also face danger in today's world, as do bank tellers and schoolteachers. Now, when you talk about the #1 chance of meeting a violent death— well then, yes cops do lead the pack in that dubious distinction. What a bummer. I'm gonna try to beat that one.

These are just a few, but let's face it—the myth is always more fun. Now about that free stuff. Hello? Anybody?

Taking the Test

One of the most common questions I get is about the testing process and steps involved in being hired as a peace officer. Indeed it is tedious, difficult and lengthy. It should be.

The first step is the written test. Usually two hours in length, it is a general knowledge test with portions covering math, language and logic. Believe it or not, this is the easy part.

Once you have passed the written test with a fixed minimum score, you advance to the oral interview. This is probably the most intimidating portion of testing to most applicants—a face-to-face, up close chat with up to five cops. Before you are done, you will be convinced they did not believe anything you said.

Usually these teams are comprised of stiff-faced, seasoned, veteran officers and a supervisor. The questions are designed to test your skill at communication under pressure. Not so much what you say, but how smoothly and confident it comes out.

Questions involving law enforcement scenarios are asked, not to test your knowledge of police tactics, but your common sense and maturity. Questions regarding use of force—including deadly force—are used to judge not whether you know when or how to use force, but whether you would be sensible in applying it. While indeed nerve-wracking, this thirty to forty-five minute interview really helps in selecting those applicants truly cut out for this work.

If successful in the interview, the next step is usually a medical exam, including a urine screen for drugs, blood tests and sometimes an x-ray of the spine or lungs. Once the Doc says you're healthy, many agencies require a physical agility test to measure your fitness to perform the usual tasks of a street cop. Distance running, sprinting, strength, agility and speed are tested, along with specific tasks of perhaps changing a tire, dragging an injured person from a building and even the ability to reach all controls of a patrol car can be tested.

Okay. So far so good. We will assume you are still in the running!

Next, is the psychological testing portion—both written testing and an interview with a police psychiatrist. For obvious reasons, this testing is crucial. It is NOT to determine if you're nuts, but rather if your personality is suited to police work. Some of the questions—about 1,500 of them on the written portion—are bizarre and humorous, but apparently reveal things about you. Just answer them without laughing. They don't like it when you laugh. As far as the interview—you are on your own. I haven't a clue what they're after. Just don't laugh.

Finally, after a possible polygraph examination, your background is scrutinized intensely to include interviews with your neighbors, past employers, co-workers, parents, siblings and even schoolteachers. College transcripts are verified; multiple credit histories and visits with property owners also take place.

Then, if you scored high enough, you find yourself in the police academy taking a lot more tests. Up to six months later—if all goes well—you are given a badge and sworn in.

You have earned the trust of a community, and feel a humble pride. Cherish it.

Kindergarten for Cops

A career in law enforcement when the dreaming, studying and testing are successful, usually starts in the police academy. This is a highly anticipated step in the young cop's life—their long awaited and coveted training. This training received in the classroom is, like in many other professions, just enough to get started and then *really* learn how much you *don't* know!

Further post-academy training of several weeks or months riding with an experienced Field Training Officer is just as critical as the theories and principles discussed in the unhurried and air-conditioned comfort of the lecture hall. The academy really is kindergarten for cops. Without it, advancing to "first grade" would be out of the question.

Basic training is usually from three to six months long—a mixture of classroom, physical training and practical exercises. Basic training classes will go into everything from professional orientation to constitutional law. Criminal law, traffic law and civil law will also be covered. Rules of evidence, powers of arrest, and the laws governing searches and seizures and the regulations covering game and fish are explained and discussed.

Some topics receive more intense coverage as you might imagine. Some of these are the use and upkeep of firearms, techniques of surviving and winning armed combat, custody control, hand-to-hand pain compliance techniques and the rules governing use of force. All peace officers must pass this portion with very high marks to become certified. A perfect score—100%—is mandatory on the test for use of force.

More recent training includes pursuit driving liability, just as instruction on blood born pathogens and ways to avoid contracting them when we must handle and help bloody victims, suspects or bodies—any one of which could easily have hepatitis, HIV or AIDS.

All cops become certified as Medical First Responders as part of this training. Some become approved for trucking inspections for driver health and fatigue, logs and documentation, as well as classes in livestock law. Of course, the use of RADAR adds to the academy experience—with almost another full week of learning to use this tool of enforcement.

It is true that in generations past, old salty training officers used to tell recruits immediately after shaking hands on their very first day of patrol, "*First thing I want you to do, is forget everything they taught you at the academy.*" Thankfully, today's training officers understand that without this solid foundation of knowledge provided by the exceptional instructors and guest lecturers at all police academies, the level of safety we now provide for our nation would be impossible.

On to second grade—the Field Training Officer.

The Field Training Officer

"Hot damn—let's go catch some bad guys! Who do we get to arrest first?" That was me—some nineteen years ago, on my very first day as a Wyoming State Trooper.

"Well, you can do what you want, I guess, but if you don't have me in front of a cup of coffee in five minutes, YOU'RE FIRED!" That was him, some nineteen years ago on my very first day as a Wyoming State Trooper.

When recruit officers finally graduate the months-long classroom experience of the academy, so much sunshine has pumped into them they truly think that no one would ever lie to them, run from them or try to hurt them. Then, the real world comes at them full speed and they must have a seasoned and skilled teacher at their side to calm them down, bring them back to reality, keep them correct legally and, in some cases, to keep them alive.

The overall single most important function of the Field Training Officer—a temporary assignment in some agencies, a permanent assignment in others—is to bring some reality into the fresh green life of the rookie cop. First, he or she will look the recruit over and do such simple things as check their "Batbelt" and advise them, "No, Ralph, the extra bullets go *here*, in front, where you can get to them, not in back." Or, "Okay Becky, let's try putting your handcuffs in the pouch *unlocked* this time, so we don't break the suspect's wrists when we slap them on."

A good training officer can make this instruction go smoothly in such a way as to avoid embarrassing the recruit in front of the other veterans—the group they want so badly to fit into. He or she will protect the rookie with their life, and that includes from other cops. Although understanding, veteran cops can be cold-blooded to new kids, and are always looking for new "FNG" stories to pass around.

Once in the field and engaged in answering calls and making traffic stops, the Field Training Officer will be at a paradox—to both give the recruit room to try things he has learned, but to stay close enough to yank him out of the jaws of disaster should things go badly. And in law enforcement, they can go badly almost instantly.

A good FTO will use every moment he and his recruit are together—from six weeks to six months, depending on the agency—to impart everything he has learned on the job. He or she will unselfishly give everything to the rookie, knowing that one day soon that officer will "solo" and be on their own and will draw from that training to perhaps save their own life.

I have served as a Field Training Officer many times over my career, and have taught hundreds of recruits at the academy. With each recruit entrusted to me, I have always offered this:

"Get me in front of a cup of coffee in five minutes, or YOU'RE FIRED!"

The Badge

Some time ago while teaching at the Wyoming Law Enforcement Academy I was asked by a recruit why some badges had several very sharp points like mine and others were rounded or oval shaped.

"Well, the sharp ones," I said, "are to remind us of how badly it will hurt when it is shoved down our throat!"

"And the rounded ones?" asked the recruit.

"Well, those are worn by the more enlightened departments," I said with a smile. "See, in their early days, the 'Big Chiefs' in some of those departments may have had that happen to *them* and learned that rounded might go down easier—so they ordered them!"

Kidding aside, any cop on the job for a few years no matter the agency, learns very quickly what the badge is and, more importantly, what it is *not*.

First is its size. Far to small to hide behind, we learn to stand on our own and that the respect we must earn should go to *us*, not the badge. It is merely a *symbol* of our authority—not the authority itself.

The number on the badge reminds us of or accountability to you, and our place in the department as only one of many people who get the job done.

The quick, simple mechanism on the back allows easy removal from a soiled shirt, and this serves to remind us of how swiftly and easily our administrators remove the few bad apples who manage to slip through the web of our hiring screens, and who would try to soil the sanctity of our profession.

The name of our agency boldly emblazoned and sometimes encircling around the state seal, clearly demonstrates our overall mission—to protect our state and its people.

The image of golden or platinum metal is just that—an image. The reality is that it is only plated metal. The message here is clear. Inside, we are flawed and regular people with all of the imperfections God has given everyone else. It is the ability and strength to overcome these weaknesses and fears which can boost us up to the higher standards and moral conduct expected not just of police officers, but of all civilized and honorable citizens.

The slight weightiness of my badge tells me everyday of how hard I worked to get it and how prized it is to hold. Finally, it reminds me how sad the day will be when I retire and have to give it back. A younger new professional will pin it on and, I hope, keep it clean.

In the end, I hope he or she will remember that the badge will not make a cop glitter; but that it is the cop who makes the badge shine!

No Boundaries

When is a cop not a cop? This is a question asked from time to time when jurisdictional boundaries come into play. Jurisdiction is loosely addressed in the criminal statutes but more clearly defined in criminal procedure law.

Indeed, under NORMAL conditions a city Police Officer, for example, would not have police powers in another city. But if requested for assistance by another peace officer, or if assigned for temporary duty by the Chief of Police, full powers exist. This is allowed under specific law. However...

The truth is that a cop is *always* a cop. We are sworn to act whenever a need is brought to our attention wherever we are, twenty-four hours a day, seven days a week. We cannot and would not just slam the door and say, "I'm off. I can't help you. Call somebody else." Our oath, and hopefully our ethics, just will not let that happen. Perhaps our help might be limited to notifying the proper authority, or as intense as stopping a crime in progress, but we WILL always help you. A good cop really has no boundaries and no clock.

Having said that, here's how it works. The municipal police officer is the authority within the legal limits of his city. They can enforce all city ordinances, state statues, municipal regulations and civil obedience rules from their mayor. In this respect, their authority is wider than a deputy sheriff or state trooper, as the latter two cannot enforce city ordinances unless specifically cross-sworn.

A sheriff or his deputy has county wide jurisdiction, including all incorporated cities, with regard to state law and county ordinances and, specifically, to county property within municipalities like the county fairgrounds. In these cases, this is sometimes a shared jurisdiction with the municipal police. Further, the sheriff and his deputies are the official servant of the courts, serve civil process and act as bailiffs. The sheriff is the keeper of all criminals convicted for crimes in the county and is the ultimate authority in providing for their welfare. Finally, the sheriff is traditionally the enforcement official for all county taxes.

State troopers and special investigative agents of a state's Division of Criminal Investigation have complete state police powers throughout the entire state including all counties and all cities. These state-level peace officers have no authority to enforce city ordinances, county ordinances, or, in the case of state troopers, may not serve civil process. Otherwise, they are fully empowered to perform any general policing needs they are called to at any time at the direction of the Governor.

Other law enforcement officials like Game and Fish Wardens, prison and correctional officers, school police, brand inspectors, deputy fire marshals, and state park rangers, have "limited" powers, either in what laws they enforce, or a limit of powers as to when they are actually "on the clock."

Whether in their jurisdiction or just passing through on a family vacation, whomever they work for or whatever words are emblazoned on their badge, each will protect you with their life.

Isn't that what really matters?

When You're Cool

Cool is mandatory in police work. Cool under pressure and … well … just cool. Most police officers take pains to ensure the "squared away" look of polished leather, straight "gig" lines (that's the matching line up of the zipper and shirt button flap), and uniforms without a speck of lint—not to mention a stain from the soup they had for lunch yesterday.

Cool also has to do with style and grace in contacts with people. Be assured that the vernacular and inflections uttered by police to some guy walking down the dark alley behind your home at 3:00 AM is quite different than that used in a passing visit with a business owner at midday on his downtown foot beat. The cool in these two scenarios is quite different.

Cool while scared to death is a clearly unspoken message to the bad guy that whatever happens in that contact—whatever stupid thing the bad guy is thinking of trying—has already been calculated and resolved in the officer's mind and the bad guy knows he will lose.

The other cool is, well, just cool, because it's just cool to stand there in a shiny, pressed uniform and glossy, squeaky and polished leather looking good. Yes indeed.

There is one accessory the officer can use to accentuate not only the cool factor, but also the officer's mystery and utter confidence. By simply wearing them, the cool goes up three points. This one thing has always been standard apparel for all uniformed cops and, in fact, should probably be issued on day one right along with his gun belt and handcuffs. Have you guessed? Shades, man! Sunglasses.

Some shades are truly the throwaway or "drop" shades you can pick up at any corner convenience store. You try on about twenty pairs in the little mirror they offer and then you look like a dork with the tag hanging down between your eyes. But, they're cheap. You drop $5—$10 and you are good to go. Until they scratch—usually in about an hour.

At the other end of the "spectrum," some specks require a small fortune and an A+ credit rating just to think about buying. $500 for non-prescription sunglasses? Are you *nuts*? And they're *plastic*?

Somewhere in-between there are some pretty good specks for everyone else, but to a cop they have to be just right. Not too mean, but very, very dark. And no mirrored lenses. Those are usually against department policy.

Only two brands meet all required pricing, safety, styling, and "cool" specifications for cops. Ray Bans and Gargoyles. That's it—just those two. Dark gray—the darker the better. The kind that make you look like an alien with huge black eyes.

Finally, they must be worn at all times—24/7—yes, even at night. Why?

Because when you're cool, the sun shines *ALL* the time!

Home Sweet Home

A cop's home is more than a house. It is, in the mind of a police officer, a castle with a moat and drawbridge. It matters not if it's an old, broken-down singlewide trailer, a cheesy apartment, or the finest house on the block. For the cop it is sanctuary. It is safe. Life is good here. Clean and wholesome.

You see, there are moments in a cop's working life lasting seconds or days, where everything they love becomes buried deep in their mind. It's still there, buried underneath the collection of scenes from the unpleasant to the unthinkable and horrific. Their hopeful and optimistic view of life is stuffed in the subconscious, hiding from moments of sheer terror and deep sadness.

Imagine holding a child in the last few moments of life after a crash. Or watching the vocally, mournful grief when you to knock on a door at 3:00 AM and, after frightening the family standing there half-asleep in their pajamas, informing them of a death of a loved one. Consider rummaging through the twisted remains of cars, only to find and touch severed body parts—actually inspecting them up close for telltale markings and clues as to what happened.

Nothing spoils the innocent picture of domestic bliss like jumping between fighting spouses, only to be beaten and cut yourself for trying to help. The image of an evening of good cheer at some friendly bar is dissolved when police are called to fights involving alcohol. Fights nearly always involve alcohol.

And rather than turn away from all this negative "karma," they must look forward, directly at it, wade in it and deal with it. They must touch it, smell it and solve its mystery. They have no buck to pass. This is their duty to you. It is what you pay them to do.

Over time these events and the resulting moral and spiritual doubts, serve well to create a hardened shell—a "crust". But even deeper, underneath that crust, these scenes completely and forever reverse opinions, alter perceptions and change priorities. Whatever innocence and naivety is brought to the job is rapidly eaten away and, without a balance—a safe haven where these events do not happen—hope will be irretrievably lost.

Most veteran police officers I know keep their home as far away from police work as possible. No scanners, no "World's Scariest Chases" on television, and no "cop talk."

But at the forefront of their thoughts and planning, working their way into the equation before each traffic stop, before each domestic call, before arriving at each felony in progress and each bar fight, is the vision of home. Home sweet home, and ensuring they make it back there.

I say to you here and now, the picture of my castle, my queen and our children, have kept me alive and have given me dauntless courage when I was afraid to the core. They and our home are not the reason for my armor—they *are* my armor.

Now ... if I could just afford to stock the moat with trout!

Our Humanity—Sometimes a Bitter Pill

Today I washed laundry in preparation for a week away from the family. I am going to an in-service school, where among other things the members of my agency will be reminded of ethical standards, good morals and our responsibility to be shining examples to humanity.

I stopped folding my clothes for a moment to read the *Casper Star-Tribune*, the largest statewide newspaper in Wyoming. As I read, I was shocked to learn of a Wyoming peace officer recently charged with sexual assault. By coincidence, my column also appeared in that paper on the same day and sung praises of Wyoming Cops.

While I stand firm on my words, I wonder—is news like this as bad as it seems to me? Is it the broad brush I worry about, or does the public understand? Do they understand this guy is an anomaly—an isolated freak in the selection process who slipped by the background and psychological testing?

We in law enforcement understand too well the implicit damage done to your confidence in us when stories like these become public. Just like the thousands of excellent doctors out there who fear an expose about quacks on *60 Minutes*, the occasional story of a cop gone bad makes us cringe that it might reinforce an inner fear some have of police. Or worse, rekindle a suspicion.

In the United States there are 750,000 sworn cops with various agencies. Other than the one or two you read about, the rest do it right and do it with honor. As a member of that majority, I am saddened when these stories see print. And angered.

Born to Catch Dirt Bags

Understand this about cops: To be successful in this business a man or woman must have an innate gut desire to risk danger, and a completely insatiable curiosity. While most people see oddities and simply shrug their shoulders, courteously minding their own business, cops react in just the opposite manner. They look closer, deeper and farther—not looking away, but staring. This core curiosity is something one is either born with, or not. Either it's there or it isn't. And in a cop, at least one who is content and successful, it is there. In fact, two bags full!

Almost from infancy, the man or woman destined to wear a badge will be inclined not to be afraid of strangers, but to be intrigued by them. Nervous parents will constantly be diverting the attention of their little boy or girl away from the scary or suspicious looking citizen they see standing in a crowd. But when that child wants to look, take it as a warning—you may have a cop on your hands! And if he utters the words "dirt bag" before the age of four, there is no doubt. This is a cop.

Children who become cops, statistically, are usually first-born children in a home where they were given responsibilities over other children at a young age. Many were children who took charge and were leaders in their group of playmates. They often stood up for the weaker or younger who were being picked on by bullies or being teased.

In contrast to a generation ago, most cops have college degrees and always had a specific goal of becoming a professional peace officer. In generations past, a cop became a cop mostly as a way to earn a paycheck and decent benefits without the need to attend college. In today's world the competition is strong and deep for a law enforcement career, and the completion of post secondary education is not only advantageous, but also required by many agencies.

Of course, the true beneficiaries of today's force of professional peacemakers are you—the citizens who pay the salaries and provide the equipment we need. Your businesses and homes are patrolled using specifically designed patrol tactics and researched indices of trouble. Crimes committed against you are investigated with the tenacious and meticulous attention to both the obvious—and more so—the latent evidence which might have been overlooked ten years ago. While no less dedicated, police forces in past generations had not yet learned many of the scientific clues at hand, nor had they been given the training and equipment needed to pursue them.

Finally, today's police officer brings you something more. Subjecting themselves to difficult written and verbal testing, an extensive background investigation, credit check, polygraph, drug screening and psychological testing, these educated men or women, if fortu-

nate enough to be one of the ten percent of applicants to make it through this screening process, looked away from a myriad of higher paying careers for which they qualify with a clear mission in mind:
To protect you, and those you love. And ... to catch dirt bags!

The Numbers Game

I am no hot dog when it comes to numbers. No supercop here, folks. Just ask any of the guys I work with and they will happily verify there is no asbestos pocket liner in my shirt pocket. My pen is only lukewarm on my craziest day, and you can bet if I write you, you had it commin'!

Like other cops, I would always prefer to give you a friendly warning than a costly citation. But sometimes that warning has no effect. In those cases when there is no other way, I am more than happy to make it official, but I assure you I am just as happy when you've learned your error and change your ways for free.

I had to laugh the other day when I had just bid farewell to a less than happy customer. After he signed his promise to handle the rather costly ticket I had just given him, he bravely shouted to me as he drove away, "YOU JUST HAD TO MAKE YOUR QUOTA, YOU #$#$*$*$&.....!" He truly had the wrong guy.

Assigning a number of tickets an officer must write in a shift is dubious at best, and a cheesy, unprofessional way to do business. No modern-day law enforcement agency I am aware of does this anymore. At least I hope not. In Wyoming, we are free to write as few or as many as we need to get the job done.

There is, to shelve another popular belief, no magic threshold where a cite is written versus a warning. Whether or not a motorist is warned as opposed to cited is governed by many things. And while textbooks say otherwise, the plain truth is your attitude, evidence of remorse or ignorance, equipment problems, wind, weather, other pending calls or even the officer's personal needs, *can* have an effect on this in some cases. The thing you must always remember, however, is that warnings are usually *our* idea. Not yours. If you beg for one, I assure you it does no good and it can irritate most officers. In fact, it might result in a cite when the officer was considering a warning in the first place!

The best advice I can give you is to always assume that every badge you see out there is indeed a hard case with a flaming quill. A real stickler with an overwhelming need to rid society of evildoers. A hot dog with lots of ticket books, not at all too busy to stop you, no need for a nature break with nothing better to do than write every living, breathing person on his beat. Then govern your driving accordingly! If you are stopped expect the worst, but take advantage of the second chance if you get one and correct the problem.

Understanding the truth about the human reality of law enforcement and issues such as these are key to your insight of the men and women who live among you and do this job, then go home at the end of the day just like you. Off comes the gun belt, uniform and ballistic vest, and on go the blue jeans. They become regular people, with families, barking dogs and yards to mow.

There, they deal with numbers familiar to us all. A grocery budget, rent, utility bills, insurance and school supplies. It just never ends…

Shhhh…It's a Secret

People think we cops have secrets. Secret codes, secret gestures and secret tactics. While certain knowledge is confidential and some tactical operations are less spoken of, it isn't like it's juicy stuff requiring a Super-Duper-Supreme-Ultra-Crypto-Marco-Polo-Top-Secret government clearance! It's just that with scanners, public information laws and the desire to maintain a positive relationship with the press, we only have a few tricks left up our collective sleeves that the bad guys don't know about. That element of uncertainty can ensure an officer's safety in a volatile situation, and the safety of your police should be something you not only understand—but also support.

Otherwise our language is like an open book. Take the "10-Code" for example. It is *not* a secret. I don't know who or when it was decided this was "official," but it is the one used across our state—except, where it isn't.

The 10-Code was first developed many years ago when radios were far less clear, reception was far less certain, and it allowed for better understanding of garbled radio traffic. And yes, in the days before widespread scanner use, some of the code was used to prevent comprehension by unauthorized personnel. Today, the code is far from universal and used less and less—with most police officers preferring "plain speak" radio traffic.

For example, "See the man," instead of "10-17;" "Negative," instead of "10-74," or, "Get me an ambulance," instead of, "10-52." In reality, some of the 10-Code is never used, and much of it is rarely used. Do we really still need a code for picking up paychecks, reserving motel rooms and unnecessary use of radio? Actually, that one probably should be used from time to time, with the more long-winded among us—like me!

Rookies come on the job, soon get the whole thing memorized, and just love to "talk the talk." However, seasoned and uh, "worldly" cops like me? You gotta be kidding.

Every once and again I'll nearly drive into the borrow ditch as I hurriedly search my glove box and under my seat for my copy of the official bright red card listing each 10-Code as some rookie rattles off three or four in a row. Then he sounds professional and cool, while I sound like a dork, as I try to reply.

Usually my panicked answer comes out translated as something like, "Okay. You go back and send a drivers license to the slick roads, while I take a coffee break with lights and siren in this here fire wrecker!"

There is an "8 code" for road conditions and a "9 code" for weather—again—not because it's a secret, but to simplify and clarify the message. Me? I just call the roads, "Greasy" or "Extremely greasy!" And to me, visibility is described as either, "Can't see past the windshield," or, "Can't see past the hood ornament!"

There are codes for places we may be when out of the car, like our office, the hospital, a meal break or court. Again, some of us just say it, others use the code for it—sounds cool but there's really no need. Do you really want to know the code for "Big Bob's Greasy, Good and Sloppy Hamburger Joint?" Don't ask me—I couldn't tell you. But there is one I think.

Finally, there are codes we use when we go home at the end of a shift, thankful for a community at peace and for our personal survival. To some, the code is a snuggle of their kids or hug of their spouse. Others might go work in the garden or crack a cold one, put the feet up and watch a late movie. While not verbal, these codes are varied but mean precisely the same thing:

"Thank you, God. I made it home again."

Starsky and Hutch

Every now and again we get a look. Often it comes from a young child, but sometimes it comes from a grownup. A full-grown person who silently wonders if our daily work life is like—well—like on TV. After you compare paychecks with the six digits per week the actor receives, there are a few other differences as well. But Starsky and Hutch it ain't.

Although we never walk up to felons and give drop-dead one-lines like, "Go ahead … make my day," evoking laughter and emotion from an unseen audience eating popcorn and relishing our next fight sequence, we do get to arrest bad guys now and again. And while they are fearless of the danger as they shoot up everybody once a week just in time for commercials, we do often have to act brave when inside we are trembling so badly we know it shows. And not to burst any bubbles, but no cop I ever knew got to chase people through malls and destroy several patrol cars and sidewalk vendor carts. We do sometimes get into a short pursuit, but road spikes end them very quickly.

Unless we can afford a few days off without pay, we don't roll our eyes and ignore our commanding officers (at least when they can see us). No way. I have never been so mad as to toss my $600 department-issued sidearm out the window of a fast moving car because I ran out of bullets. Pretty dull, huh?

Can my car really make those fifty-foot jumps like in San Francisco chase scenes and never destroy the frame, much less loose a hubcap or bash my head on the roof? Nope.

Folks, I have never had a deep emotion-filled chat with a partner. If I did the laughter from the squad room would be deafening. No, I do not have an endless string of snitches I pay $20 each for the information that will single-handily solve a case I have been struggling with. No cop you have ever known has such an endless supply of cash.

I never get free meals. Never. I will not say there is no such thing as a "police discount," but I can tell you it's nowhere *I'm* privy to! But oh yes—yes indeed—occasionally someone will buy us a cup of coffee or soda pop. Relax—it's just a very thoughtful and traditional gesture—not a payoff.

Several years ago, there was a line in a movie wherein an elder Asian gentleman is teaching an East Coast teenager karate, because several other rich kids who have learned the art from an evil instructor are picking on him. At one point the wise old man is asked by the youngster about cool moves and techniques and stuff he would like to learn, like punching through walls and leaping ten feet into the air, only to do a triple-gainer-back-flip-jackknife-twist triple kick on his attacker!

"You ... you too much TV!" says the wise karate master.

Indeed.

Ralph

This is a story about a cop named Ralph. In two decades on the street, never have I known anyone more gallant and completely devoted. His bravery was beyond human understanding, and completely unselfish. Always ready and excited to begin another shift, Ralph loved police work as a game—a game he always won. For all of his dedication, all he ever wanted in return was simple praise for a job well done. For all the time he was around, there was never even a whisper of a doubt that Ralph would give his life to protect any one of us.

Short in stature, he truly was a paradox. Standing only twenty-six inches at the shoulder, he was the smallest but the most intimidating member of the force. Pound for pound, he was stronger than any of us—his mere presence completely immobilizing to the most violent criminal. Ralph was a police canine—one of thousands in service across the country.

German Shepard, Rottweiller, Doberman, Bloodhound, Springer Spaniel or Lab, the police canine is a marvel to watch as he reduces to minutes the work his human partners would take hours to complete.

A scent dog can smell hundreds and hundreds of distinct odors—simultaneously. While you and I smell a cheeseburger, they smell the beef, cheese, onions, ketchup, mustard, pickles and sesame seed bun separately and distinctly.

And by the way, none of those odors can effectively mask what the dog is trained to detect—drugs, dead bodies, bombs, lost children or survivors of avalanche and earthquakes. A good scent dog can completely search a car for dope in just a few minutes. The dog trained to find explosives can sniff any suspicious container in mere seconds, for the telltale odors of specific chemical compounds used in bombs—odors that are undetectable to man.

Protection and criminal apprehension is another task our tail wagging friends do on the job. While not naturally aggressive, this task is all just a big game to them. Animals used in law enforcement, notwithstanding the movie industry, are NOT trained to be vicious or mean. In fact, to be considered for police training, all candidates must prove they are NOT prone to bad temperament.

A simple demonstration will convince anyone of the good nature of these dogs. When given the command to be on alert, the police canine will protect his handler with his life and chase down and bite a fleeing suspect if need be. This "bite" is not intended to rip the arm or leg to shreds, but is used merely as a clamp—to hold the suspect for his human handler. The demonstration will show that at the instant the command to "stop the game" is given to the animal, the same person the dog just chased down, tackled and bit, can wrestle and play with him, providing his reward for a job well done.

What happened to Ralph? Well, after six years of faithful service, and seventy-five felony arrests to his credit, Ralph's handler took him for a walk and tearfully thanked him. Ralph retired and enjoyed many more years of sleeping late and creating puppies.

Then, one sad day in his thirteenth year, Ralph died in his sleep. Many of us honored to have worked with him are convinced he remains curled up at God's feet, enjoying the gifts he gave his handler for so long. Peace, protection and altruistic love.

The Eyes of a Cop

In the eyes of a cop, the world never sleeps. It's a life of night shifts, weekend workers and holiday travelers, which ensures a never-ending cycle—one from which there is no respite.

In the mind of a cop, suspicion is always a key—always a part of our thoughts. People—the way they look, the way they talk, the way they act—are analyzed a thousand times a day. We silently ask ourselves why, when, how, who and where it all fits in. If it doesn't, our job is to ask more. Look farther. Probe deeper.

In the world of a cop a smile can be a signal of goodwill, or imminent attack. A shy glance can be respect, or a sign of crime afoot. A handshake can be just a friendly gesture, or used to pull us off balance. A seemingly good-natured arm around the shoulder or casual slap on the back can be the warmth of friendship, or the first strike. In our world bad things happen when least expected. So, we always expect them. And unless we see you coming, we should not be touched. You may not like the reception you get.

In the personality of a cop, suspicion, nosiness and skepticism are the finest attributes we can give our community, but if not understood their intent can be lost in their effect. Our people—the citizens we work for, can think us unsociable or aloof when the reality is we are keenly focused on their safety. To do this well, detached observations must be constant and completely objective.

In the life of a cop home becomes a safe haven—a sanctuary where the guards can be let down and the world is good and safe. Cops prefer backyard barbeques to nightclubs, jeans to slacks, and family camp outs to "social gatherings." Our precious time at home becomes so much more than just time to eat and mow the grass. It renews all that we hold priceless. It heals the emotional wounds inflicted each day on the job.

Two Seconds

An elderly woman calls 911 screaming for help and says something unintelligible about a man with a knife in her house. The last thing your dispatcher hears is a blood-curdling scream to hurry. Then the phone goes dead. This information is relayed to you by radio, and your heart starts pumping wildly. You call for backup and you drive lights and siren as fast as you can to the address given, screeching to a halt on the street. Now what do you do?

Expecting trouble you hurry to the door, gun in hand and ready to act. Suddenly, the front door bursts open and an elderly man runs out the door with blood-soaked clothing and a bloody butcher knife in hand. He sees you and turns—running toward you! Now what do you do? You have two seconds to decide…Now one second. He is now within reach of you with that twelve-inch knife. What do you do? You are dead if you hesitate or make the wrong choice.

Did you shoot him to save your own life? If so, you just started ten years of civil suits, possible criminal prosecution, and a gauntlet of humiliation and questioning for your family. Because, you see, you just shot an innocent man. He was butchering his elk and cut his wrist severely—that's why his wife called 911. In his panic, he ran out to meet the ambulance he thought was coming. He ran to you for help before he passed out. And you shot him. No one will understand. Not a soul on earth—except maybe a cop who has been there.

You and I, reading this story the next day in the morning paper, can sip our coffee in our warm, cozy home, lean back and put our feet on the coffee table and contemplate the story in the paper. We can, just like the media and courts, second-guess the officer to our heart's content. In our comfortable surroundings we talk to our family, and perhaps our friends throughout the day at work. And in friendly discussion, voice our non-official opinions of the officer's actions. We have all day.

That officer had two seconds.

Scenarios like this can happen at any time of day or night and with any number of variables. The decision to shoot or not, to use a nightstick or pepper spray, or risk injury with hand-to-hand combat techniques, are usually made within seconds of perceiving a threat. Right or wrong, we live or die with the decision we make.

Sometimes, on very rare occasions, that decision results in the death or injury of someone mistaken as a person the police officer thought was going to kill either him or you. How will you react to a story like this? Please understand that in addition to the pain for the family of the victim involved, this event will scar and emotionally maim the officer and *his* family for the rest of their lives. With almost 100% certainty, his career was over at the instant it happened, but he will linger for years trying to overcome the guilt and get on with his life. But soon, his career will end.

If he is fortunate and is not prosecuted for manslaughter, he will still be sued for money he does not have in civil court. He will never again have a "normal" life. Never.

You have every right to expect exemplary standards in your police, and we try. We really try. But if you expect perfect judgment; raw, selfless courage and flawless results, please keep in mind that sometimes all we have are two seconds.

Just about the time it takes to read this sentence.

Today's Cop

Honestly, when you walked out the door this morning to go and do whatever it is that you do, did you look back over your shoulder at the good things in your life? Did you glance around the yard, scratch the dog's head and silently give thanks to God? Are you amazed at the immense goodness your life has come to stand for? Today's cop does. Every day.

Did you sneak out of the house in the wee hours to oversee the safety of everyone else, trying not to wake your spouse? Did you take just a moment to peek at the deeply sleeping, peaceful body under the crumpled blankets—whispering a promise to the one person who truly understands the hype versus the real deal? A promise that you will come home—no matter what? A cop does. Every single day.

And honestly, did you slip into the rooms of your sleeping children and through the thick darkness strain happily to see their faces and hear the soft music of their dreamy breathing? With a humble smile, did you bend down and kiss the cheek of a little person who thinks you are a God? Today's cop does. Every day—without fail.

Are you constantly aware of surroundings—constantly scanning a room? Are your friends chosen carefully, and treasured because they understand? Is the world after midnight something you understand too well? Do you know where to get a cup of fresh coffee at 4:30 in the morning?

Do you regularly practice methods to kill or injure another? Do you anticipate an attack from every stranger you meet? Do you rehearse a plan for escaping and winning that attack? Do you study civil, criminal, and traffic law daily—without a law degree? Do you know death? Have you touched another life merely by your presence? This is the life of a cop. Today's cop.

Many have tried, but few have actually worn a badge. Many talk the talk, but few have walked the walk. Those who have only talked have romantically envisioned pointing a deadly weapon at another human being just itching for reason to shoot. Those who walk the walk hope to God it never happens. And when it does, they are more often than not devastated beyond repair. The talkers think they could brush it off. The walkers know better.

In that job you do, what are the two most important days of your career? A promotion? A raise? To cops it is the day they are hired and the day they retire. The years in-between are a mixture of terror and fun, depression and elation. They can be exciting or boring, lightning-fast or slow. Nevertheless, in the end, when the day finally arrives and he is still alive and healthy, the veteran is ready. Ready to hang it up and move on to a new life where suspicion can be set aside for trust, and where some other person can live that life.

A cop's job is full of honor and pride, and the profession today enjoys a hard-earned prestigious standing in the community. At times this is tested by reports from across our country of cops gone bad, but I can assure you the rest of the cops of today—your cops—are more offended and angered at these reports than you will ever be. The cop of today—your cop of today—is a shining example of professional discipline, classroom knowledge, and street-smart skill. He or she speaks both the vernacular of the most vial criminal, and that of a legal scholar. This is what you demand.

Today's cop. He can deliver your baby, or deliver you from evil. Not bad for a human!

The Code of Silence

A popular myth about cops is a "code of silence." Some mythical pledge taken I assume by blood, where cops swear—all 750,000 of us—to never tell of the mean and nasty things we are constantly scheming to do to the innocent citizens we serve.

A legal scholar you may remember from a high profile trial claimed we are trained in the academy to not talk, and to lie on the witness stand! All of us! I must have cut class that day because I missed that lecture. The only one I remember was the one where we learned of exactly what kind of gutter-slime we were if we did anything but tell the complete truth. That one I remember—and agree with.

It is true that any profession (including law, medicine, engineering or science) that recruits from the human race is going to be infected from time to time. And these "viruses" should be dealt with severely and quickly. No professional peace officer would disagree.

Having said that, know that there are indeed some covert facets to police work. Some, especially tactical and those based upon the use of intelligence and undercover activity, are necessarily kept quiet. No, not to deceive the public or to somehow subvert the constitution. To protect you and us from organized crime, narcotics, and the violence that is always in the same room with the people involved in them. And torture and death should an undercover agent or informant be identified. So yes…that stuff is kept quiet.

Other than that aspect of this profession, police work is out there for all to see. That's why we log every step we take, report everything we see and document every action. We wear a distinct and clearly identifiable uniform, with our name proudly emblazoned on a shiny plate above the pocket. We talk on publicly monitored radios, drive overtly marked cars, even have publications, websites and even a few newspaper columns! If I'm hiding anything it's news to me.

Secrets? Why do we allow journalists and even interested citizens to ride along and see what we do on any given shift? Take a ride with us! In short order, I am confident you will see a world you never knew was out there. You'll also see we aren't a bunch of secret agents with genuine decoder rings and watch radios, seeking out the next secret we can keep from you. We are men and women, moms and dads, children and siblings, with zits and sometimes gas. We are imperfect humans with a job requiring utter perfection, lest our efforts be dissected and criticized from every angle.

Unlike the people in that attorney's imagination, we haven't the time nor desire to keep the real world from you. Only the courage and skill to keep it from harming you. We cuss, and are perhaps on occasion gruff and harsh, with seemingly little time or longing to engage you in a deep, meaningful conversation. I assure you there is usually a reason.

I suggest that perhaps that reason, sometimes, is as simple as our last call. Perhaps a child was tortured; perhaps a woman was beaten. Forgive us, but sometimes we just cannot talk about it. We just can't.

The Special Cops

The first thing I can tell you about special reactionary units is that I can't tell you much about special reactionary units. For many reasons the identities of members and their tactical methods are kept quiet and confidential. In this small way we attempt to stay one step ahead of the bad guys.

These teams are called many things—the title is usually an acronym; *SWAT*, for Special Weapons and Tactics; *STAR*, for Special Tactics and Response; *SRT*, for Special Response Team; *CERT*, for Crisis and Emergency Response Team; *SOS* for Special Operations Squad, and the list goes on and on. No matter what they are called, assignment to these teams is highly coveted, as membership clearly testifies to their dedication and skill. It is the zenith of the police profession and the members are held in utmost respect.

On any such team the individual members each have specific tasks they train extensively for, and several secondary functions for which they cross-train. While each component of these teams is critical, they are designed in such a manner as to allow for injuries, absence or otherwise being short a member or two.

The entry team is comprised of several members; all of whom train with a single mission in mind. To be ready and equipped to breach and enter any building, vehicle or other dwelling, to rescue hostages, stop armed assaults or forcibly arrest the most desperate and violent of criminals. While certain weapons and tools are used as needed, it is raw and focused courage, physical strength, conditioning and a selfless willingness to risk a hit in saving lives, which distinguish the entry team members.

The hostage negotiator is another crucial component of special teams. The skill they have is verbal communication, compassionate understanding and a unique ability to remain completely calm and collected—in fact sometimes seemingly jovial or lighthearted—knowing all the while that one wrong word, a pause, or even one wrong inflection could very easily push a desperate criminal to kill their hostage. Negotiators have specific and extensive training for this role and have saved countless lives.

The sniper and observer form a separate team within the response unit. The observer works closely with the sniper, and serves as an extra set of eyes to verify the target, and to watch the sniper's back as he must concentrate without distraction on his shot. To qualify as a sniper, the obvious skill required is dead-on, pinpoint accuracy and control of long-range firearms. But what might surprise you is another attribute they must have—an overwhelming value placed on human life. While there can be absolutely no hesitation if given the order or "green light" to shoot, the sniper understands that their job, if carried out, means nothing else worked to bring a bad situation under control. That everything the special unit had tried to do failed to end the confrontation with no loss of life—the ultimate goal of any team.

Yes, these are very special teams. Comprised of very, very special cops—all of whom are just part of what it takes to protect you, your family, your community and your country.

Pig

Her choice was to serve others—to protect the weak from the strong, the good from the bad, and the children from them all. And to some, she is not welcome.

He has honed his skills to provide an instrument of strength; a haven of good in a world gone crazy with violence and greed, chemical ingestion and many people devoid of values and decency. And some only question his honesty.

She keeps her uniform clean, her leather polished and her appearance groomed. Her personal life would seem lonely to some, but she keeps it this way on purpose. She must. Any attack to her character—whether based on reality or fiction—will lead to hours of explaining and denying—unlike anything her male counterparts would ever have to endure. And some, who don't understand, call her a prude.

His small children ask the most difficult questions. Why does Daddy wear a bulletproof vest? Why does he wear a gun? One day, they know. From then on, the seed of terror is planted. Always there, always dormant, never gone. Their world of fantasy and magic is somehow shorter lived than the wonderful innocence of their friends. As they grow, the ignorant bliss is replaced by a latent fear that never leaves until the day he retires. And some think he doesn't know.

His wife long ago came to understand that if their marriage was going to work she would have to give him up to the drunks, prostitutes and felons, having faith in her husband's own will to come home—to always come home—no matter what. It was futile to try to protect him from the evil. For she could not. She gives him to God and waits. And most of her friends have no idea.

He lives in a dark world of liars, cheaters, thugs and killers and fights everyday not to become cynical and hateful of society. He has seen the effects to society of too much alcohol, too much greed and too much weakness and he has come to be sickened by it but lives a paradox. His job requires him to relentlessly seek out these people. Then when he finds them and deals with them he is sickened again.

Her eyes have seen the ugliness of violent death, too many times to count. And she has placed these mental injuries in a place in her mind— a place God builds especially for a cop's spouse.

In his time, soon to end as he "pulls the pin" and takes his small pension, he has held the hands of children, of green recruits and of the old and dying. All of whom were living with a fear they had never known but came to him for comfort. He has prayed silently as he searched buildings for burglars, entered dark backyards for prowlers, and compassionately held out his hand twice to men who wanted to jump from buildings. He has served humanity with honor. Yet some still doubt his motives.

Both have seen, felt, tasted, heard and smelled the world in the way only a police officer does. In their pain and grief they have wept like children. Just like everyone else, cops hurt, need, hope and love. And some still call them, "Pig."

Chapter Two
The Cop's World

A Cop's Offering

A couple of winters ago a municipal police officer I know was working midnights and in the first two hours of his shift had already broken up a bar fight, intervened in a rather heated domestic argument, and had been scolded by an irate motorist he whacked for an unsafe turn. The moon was full, the sky crystal clear and it was cold—really cold—teetering just above freezing.

He was hungry and had just made it to a popular burger chain drive-through window before closing time. He grabbed a quick bite of dinner and a large Coke and as he drove away he enjoyed the salivating and enticing aroma of the hot fries and cheeseburger in the little brown sack on his seat. Just as he reached down with his right hand, clumsily fishing through the sack in the dark, he saw something. Up, under the girders of the interstate bridge he was passing under he saw a dark figure—a clump of something. Then he saw it move!

Quickly, he shined his spotlight up to it, and could see it was a man! The man had assembled a makeshift bed from cardboard boxes, a drop cloth and newspapers. In the light he appeared not the least bit frightened but, rather irritated at being disturbed.

After a quick interview the officer learned that while now filthy and penniless, this guy was once something else. He seemed well-educated and polite, but for reasons unknown had nothing to his name but the clothes on his back. He was clearly suffering the effects of exposure and hypothermia, and coughed so harshly the officer suggested medical attention. The man fervently refused the help. He said he just wanted to sleep a bit, and he would be moving along to the next town or train to get a ride home to the East Coast.

After running a check on the man and finding no wants or warrants (and with the man's refusal of medical help), the officer had no choice but to leave him. He knew the man would do nothing more than try to sleep in the frigid cold. He felt sorrow and pity for this one-time productive gentleman, and truly wished he could help him or give him a little hope.

The officer continued on his patrol. Later, as the first rays of early morning light cast a red hue on the eastern Wyoming horizon, he ended his tour of duty, thankfully, without any harm to himself or any of his community. Quietly, fatigued and spent, he slipped into his warm home and touched the soft faces of his sleeping children and his loving wife. Just before conscious thought slipped away, he thanked God for getting him home safely once more, and for the blessings of his life.

As the police officer surrendered to his daytime slumber, the homeless man, chilled to the bone but otherwise okay, climbed down from under the bridge and, as promised, started out on foot on the shoulder of Interstate 80.

The only trace left of him was the makeshift bedding and something else. A small brown sack containing an empty cup, a burnt French fry and three soggy pickles. He hated pickles.

Cops and Death

In law enforcement, violent, unexpected death becomes something we deal with with surprising routine and eventual calm. After a few dozen scenes of incredible devastation of the human body—be it from fire, bombs, auto crashes, vicious criminal mayhem or suicide—the dead body is just another part of the job.

Sometimes gruesome, sometimes odiferous; it is always an uneasy moment when the time comes to touch it; to put the body into a sanitary bag and load it into the coroner's Suburban. Believe it or not, this task is taken very seriously and, in fact, with reverence. I confess that I have hidden behind "black humor" to get past this. However, for the few seconds of actual contact and manipulation of the corpse, all cops I have known become quietly dignified, as care is taken to be gentle and quiet. It is as if the person can feel us, or is at least watching us.

Recently, the public has learned of the off-color dialect sometimes used by emergency response people to death. As a news reporter spoke into the camera recently on TV, a worker in the background—unaware he was on camera—shouted out to another referring to "ripe stiffs." In another, a woman could be heard referring to bodies as though a mere statistic to be recorded and nothing more.

At the scene of some traffic fatalities, bystanders have heard cops refer to "grinders." These words were never meant to be heard by anyone other than the emergency personnel on scene, because they are incredibly aloof and galling. While this vernacular is rough and cold, it is the reality of repeated dealings with death. The dead body must become just another facet of the investigation, dehumanized and skimmed over without digging into personalities and individual traits. Once we learn the body had a name and family, perhaps children and a dog, they become real and the trauma cuts deeper.

The violent death of a child tests my metal more so than anything else. It has unnerved me at times to see a relatively unharmed face and body of a soft little person, only to learn the damage and life-taking injuries are inside and cannot be seen or stopped. Wrapping your mind around the picture of a child overcome by death—killed by the actions or ignorance of another—is something nearly impossible to do. It is, however, bittersweet to see the care and gentle touch used by all when handling the lifeless little bodies we sometimes must. By the way, there is no black humor with kids. Ever.

As the months have come and gone since September 11, 2001, the television has shown police officers and firefighters dealing with the lifeless, with flags draped over the bodies of their own. I just wanted to be sure you know that in death, no matter their place or calling in life, all are respected, quietly grieved, and treated with gentle, human dignity.

Cookies and Punch

One of the less thought of aspects of law enforcement is public relations. Depending on circumstances, the term itself is both a subject and a verb. Public relations—the subject—is that collection of media and scripts designed to foster a good rapport with the people we serve. When used as a verb, it is the specific actions we take to deliver it.

One of these is the public speaking engagement. The "presentation." Whether it is an hour spent with school kids, civic groups or business leaders, what may surprise you is that it sparks foreboding. Outright fear in the hearts of some otherwise gallant men and women, who would honestly much rather be sent in to fight with ten drunken professional wrestlers, than to stand before a group of people and … uh … visit.

A cop's element is the street. He knows it, lives it and, comes to love it. Wise guys, gangsters, militants, violent felons and the mentally unstable are our kind of people and, unbelievably, it is with them we find comfort and feel in charge of the situation. It's a control thing, and we have absolutely no idea of the questions and comments you might through at us at any moment. Bad guys could care less if our leather is polished, or our uniform is pressed and spotless, but these things are imperative when we stand before you representing our agency. Never in my double-decade law enforcement career has a felon given me a nonchalant wink and helpful gesture toward my wide open trouser fly! I cannot say the same about a talk I gave to a business group recently. So much for command presence.

"Cookies and Punch" assignments, as I call them, are not something most cops eagerly anticipate. But they serve a good purpose. They bring you into our world and allow us into yours. I personally enjoy them for just that reason. But yes, I am the odd duck.

Too often a person's only contact with us is something official, like a traffic ticket or taking your report as a victim of a crime. These and other official matters are not warm and fuzzy, and do nothing to foster friendship. And so, cookies and punch does have a valuable place.

Once, while speaking to a civic assembly, I remember as I stood there sweating bullets I noticed a woman in the very front row seemingly very uncomfortable. As it happens, I move around and get quite animated when I speak, and each time I glanced down at her or walked near her she really seemed to be tense and afraid.

Later, after the presentation, I was visiting informally with a few stragglers when I saw that woman walk past—the same one who had been in the front row.

I extended my hand to her, smiled and said, "Hey, thanks for coming and listening." She stopped, but would not complete the handshake. I stood there feeling odd but did not back down. A sheepish grin finally appeared and slowly, she reached out and shook my hand. And she discovered something. I was warm and human, not at all the stoic robot she imagined.

My hope then and now is that folks like her who might be afraid, understand and embrace our humanity, and accept the friendship we offer.

Roadside Etiquette

It may have been a flashlight in your eyes, a stern admonishment, or a gentle, kind discussion on traffic stop etiquette. One thing for sure—if you did it wrong, you learned the officer was not happy!

Traffic stops are one of the three most dangerous tasks your peace officers do for you. We may be walking up to the window of someone who just robbed you at gunpoint and left in a hurry. He may assume we know, and react with violence to get away. Perhaps he is an undiscovered escapee or fugitive in a yet unreported stolen car, or the driver may be drunk, on drugs, or mentally unbalanced. Perhaps he is a member of some extremist group (yes, we have them even in Wyoming); just waiting for the badge of honor killing a cop would bring. Bottom line ... we do not and cannot know.

On the other hand, the driver may be a good-natured and cooperative citizen, supportive of law enforcement officers and understanding of our task. But you know what? We don't know what you look like. There is no class in the law enforcement academy called, "What Bad Guys Look Like 101." We have only a second or two to make an instant personality profile using your actions and demeanor. So, what can you do, or not do, to help us?

Never exit your car without being asked. Remain in your safety belt, and stay seated. It's bad enough that *we* must stand out there in traffic, without you risking your own life! Stay put!

Keep your hands in plain view at all times. We really appreciate this one, because it's hands that harm us. Nothing else can. Just hands. Try to avoid reaching under your seat or into hidden places without telling us first! We aren't "ascared" of much, but this stuff can really bring on heartburn. Best advice here; grab the steering wheel and hold on.

Avoid arguing, shouting and interfering. We know your emotions are high when we stop you, but keep in mind that one second size up. Your behavior can appear threatening or aggressive, and when it does we must react accordingly. Use the legal system to win ... not volume! Don't worry ... be happy!

Absolutely do not … no way, no how … touch any weapons you have in the car! Need I explain this one?

At night, make us happy and turn on your dome light. Again, we're not afraid; we just don't like surprises!

Chances are we will never meet under these circumstances. We hope our very presence is enough to deter problem driving. When it doesn't, we will enforce the rules—even on otherwise law-abiding citizens. Would you have it any other way?

The Strength to Leave

One of the lousiest calls we get on the job is a family fight. These calls are unpredictable and dangerous and, unfortunately, are something your police deal with on a regular basis. While society has slowly come around to call spouses who batter the criminals they truly are, there are still many who feel it is best to look the other way. Amazingly, some communities still ignore the screaming coming from next door, and pretend not to see the scars, bruises and scrapes on the faces of the victims. Shame on us.

Some people truly believe it is their right to beat their spouse and children. Not in Afghanistan—mind you—but here! The emotional scars—especially to children exposed to this—are painful, difficult to imagine, and cannot be seen on the surface. But a police officer sees them quickly, clearly and in sharp focus. His role here is truly a paradox. These little people see him as someone who can both fix everything; and the person who will take his mommy or daddy away. The cop cannot win.

When a police officer arrives at the home his job is to quickly stop the fighting and separate the parties. Sometimes, when the fight is two willing participants, it is the police who are suddenly seen as the enemy and just as quickly as a spouse is restrained from continuing to beat the other one senseless, the one being protected will turn on the police and attack them! Suddenly, the police are perceived as picking on the wife or husband, and the other moves to protect them. The first time this happens to a rookie that officer is speechless … completely befuddled.

Once tempers are cooled down a bit the police will attempt to assess who is the aggressor, who hit who first and why, and if anyone is drunk or under the influence of drugs. And guess what—somebody usually is.

On the other hand, if a one-sided battery has occurred, things are pretty clear-cut. The officer will arrest the suspected aggressor and remove them from the home. If nobody's talking, or no battery has taken place yet, the police then become skillful negotiators and marriage counselors, trying to find a solution to the problem. Almost always this involves one party or the other leaving for the night so that both can cool off.

If the officer suspects violence will continue once the police are gone, or that harm will come to any children in the home, he has the statutory authority under domestic violence and family protection statutes to remove the children and place them in protective custody. Further powers allow the officer to forcibly remove the party felt to be the aggressor. In this day and age, we never just leave. Somebody gets a ride.

Stopping domestic violence and all that goes with it is part of our job. But it is truly the part we hate the most. To see grown adults in this state of rage and hopelessness, compounded with the use of one chemical or another, becomes a disgusting nuisance. While our hearts ache for the victim, we always clear from domestic calls knowing that while we may have prevented disaster, we have fixed nothing.

My prayer, for the beaten spouses and their children, is for peace and healing. And the confident strength to leave.

Guns and Maalox

To a cop guns are a unique contradiction. In our hands they are an instrument of life. To save ours, or the lives of our people. In the hands of bad guys, they are the instruments of death they were designed to be. A gun, particularly a handgun, has but one purpose folks—to kill. So, you can understand our trepidation when we find one concealed or within rapid reach of citizens we contact. Heartburn and two slugs of extra strength Maalox usually follow such a discovery, and it really ruins our day.

In recent years Wyoming, along with many other states, made it much easier for regular folks to carry guns concealed on their person. And many have taken advantage of the law, and now legally do so for their own protection. Some cops I know have no problem with this—especially with women who travel or otherwise find themselves alone and vulnerable in their daily lives. Others hate it and think, arguably, that only cops should have guns. In a perfect world perhaps that is how it should be. But, and this is a really big but, last time I looked we humans were far from divine flawlessness. No matter what, even when done within the spirit and letter of the law, this issue still bugs us. We can't help it. Guns really creep us out.

See, if we contact you by traffic stop or on the street, chances are we will not know you. We will not know your habits, your mannerisms, your vernacular or your state of mental stability—not to mention your opinion of cops! Then, if we find a weapon on your person we tend to get a bit frazzled. If we find you had a permit but forgot to tell us, we will not be happy! So ...

The first rule if you plan to carry a concealed gun ... always, always tell a police officer who comes in contact with you that you're carrying and have a permit for it. The law requires it, and ... well ... doesn't it just seem to make sense? It may save you a very nasty stare, a few foul words or perhaps a gun in your face and an invitation to lay on the pavement while we get a grip, frantically turn out our pockets for more antacid and check on your record!

Next, please adhere to the limits of where you can carry. No churches, schools, airports and (believe me, I have to say this) law enforcement buildings!

There are many other limits, and you must know them and follow them or you will risk jail and/or revocation of the permit. Read every word of every document regarding your permit and please ... do what it says!

In Wyoming, our state legislature made a huge statement of confidence in Wyoming citizens when they approved this relaxed concealed weapons permit law. They recognized the need for people to protect themselves as there just aren't enough people who dress like me to go around. They granted permission to do this with very few, but very crucial rules and regulations. In many other states this is not, and will probably never be a reality, and it is nearly impossible to obtain a concealed weapon permit.

In Wyoming we accept responsibility for ourselves. We treat our neighbors with respect and still believe in long-lost traditional American values such as the right to protect our families and ourselves. And usually we pray that we never need to.

Two Friends

Sometimes my job puts me in a very uncomfortable place—a place I do not want to be. One night, as a sudden and overwhelming snowstorm came through the Red Desert, I was called to the scene of a crash near a small village named Table Rock. All that I was told was that it was two big rigs, and total road blockage of the westbound lanes.

As I came closer traffic was slowing to a crawl, and soon enough I saw the crash. Two trucks were involved. They were totaled, and what was once a passenger car was merely a crumpled metal chassis—unrecognizable as to the make or model. I met with one of the truck drivers in the thick, wet, pouring snow, and she told me two women were trapped in the car with broken legs and other trauma. I rushed to the one door I could open and stuck my frozen face inside. What I saw caught me speechless and completely off balance for just a few seconds.

I knew them. Both of them. As happens from time to time in rural law enforcement, we sometimes come into official contact with friends and neighbors. Sometimes it is the unpleasant enforcement of traffic law, sometimes it is domestic issues and sometimes it is a crash. In this case it was two, dedicated professional teaching assistants who had helped in the education of my children. Both had kids of their own I had known since kindergarten. Both were in shock and horrific fear, not to mention the pain from their injuries. I did my best to reassure them and answer their questions. But I felt woefully inept and, as unprofessional as this is, emotionally connected. Sorry, but it happens. Thank God their husbands arrived on scene. I was glad for the women, as well as myself. Detached again, I completed the investigation.

As I write this, they are undergoing or are about to undergo surgical repairs and will start the process of living with the emotional aftermath such trauma brings out. Depending upon the specifics, recovery and rehab can take months to years, and even longer for the emotional baggage. I know. I have truly been there. I am still there.

As it happens these two have worked with Mrs. Geeting for many years, and she too had a connection with their kids. They were her students. The kids were still at school for basketball practice, and it was up to Mrs. G to deliver the news. She took care of everything and arranged for overnight care, relieving one worry from already overwrought parents. I am incredibly blessed with her.

Several years ago at a school musical there had been a role for three adults to sing a song with the kids. These two women and a great big funny lookin' state trooper signed up and gave what was not quite a Grammy-caliber performance. It was, however, a display shown to the student body of our love and enjoyment of little people. We had—all three of us—connected not in the detached way of a public servant and citizens, but in the way neighbors, parents and community members connect—through our children.

As I peered into that destroyed car my armor disappeared. I saw no victims, no drivers or passengers, and no statistics to record.

I saw two friends and it broke my heart.

The Crust

Recently a rookie trooper—a peach-fuzzed kid, fresh out of school with a criminal science degree and everything—was feeling overwhelmed by the job. He was assigned to five fatal crashes in *two weeks*. Some cops don't even work one in *five years*! He's been thinking he doesn't really like all of this "glory." He actually may leave the job. He hasn't developed his "crust" yet.

After his most recent fatal he was on his way home in the late afternoon when he stopped at a convenience store for a cold drink. Emotionally spent and unaware of the wisps of dried blood on his pants and shirt (from one of the victims he'd help load into the coroner's wagon), he thought he'd just grab a quick drink for his long drive home. Just as he reached the door a man approached him and angrily said, "What the heck are you doing here? I pay my taxes, and I don't pay you guys to sit around and drink soda!" This was the first time in a twelve-hour day that this officer had been able to "sit around" and drink a soda. He'd had no lunch, no breaks. He had seen three very dead people that day, two of them children. The blood on his pants was from a little, five-year-old hand still grasping a soft little Elmo.

"Write a letter to your congressman, Bub," the officer responded. He never even looked at the man. He just turned around and left. A three page letter found its way to the Governor two days later.

Would you have seen him "sitting around drinking soda?" Could you have known that earlier he was throwing up in an alley just a few blocks away after seeing the graphic ugliness of death, one more time than he needed? Have you ever seen an officer taking his "lunch" break at 3:00 AM, only to quietly slip into his dark home, pick up and hold his own sleeping child, and weep like a baby? He is a masterful actor, and no, you will not ever see him this way. In his world weakness cannot be shown. This may seem silly, but do you really want a "sensitive, emotional person" responding to your emergency?

Ours is a world unlike most people will ever know. We accept that. Understand that you do not want to see the things we respond to. The agony and terror on the faces of family and victims is real, and echoes in your mind. The blood gets on you, and the smells are sometimes truly sickening. In time a protective cover develops—a crust—not by desire, but by necessity. If the truth of what we see every day was not deflected in this way, even the best cop on the road out there would crumble.

Wouldn't you?

Two of L.A.'s Best

"If I had wanted to be popular, I would have been a firefighter." Someone very wise and experienced in the art of catching bad guys came up with that little gem many years ago. Know what? It's true. Everyone loves firefighters. Mrs. Geeting, the schoolteacher, sometimes uses the same quote on her middle school kids here in Rock Springs when they moan aloud at one of her homework lessons, or upon being held accountable for assignments.

One of my high school classmates went on to be a Los Angeles City Firefighter. His wife, Tina, was a beautiful woman full of fire and spice. Seven years ago, she became the very first female Los Angeles Police Officer to be killed in the line of duty.

While still on her training "ride-along" period, Tina and her Field Training Officer stopped to interview a group of suspicious loiterers on the side of the street. Before she could even get out of her car, she was shot in the face by one of them. Then, before he even knew he had reacted, her FTO shot and killed the assailant.

The last time I saw Tim and the kids was at the National Law Enforcement Memorial Ceremony in Washington, D.C., when together they placed a rose in the Memorial Wreath as Tina's name was read aloud to the thousands in attendance. I watched from a distance, in uniform in a sea of uniforms, hurting for all three of them. They didn't know I was there, but I was, as the representative for the Wyoming Highway Patrol.

Once, in the years before this happened, before Tina had tested for the LAPD and Timmy and I raced stock cars at the same track, we spoke briefly at his dining room table of the courage needed to be a firefighter or police officer. We each thought our own were the bravest, and Tina laughed quietly at the silliness of the conversation. Then, for a while we spoke of efficient race car cooling systems, and laughed aloud about the sheet metal I had torn from his right quarter panel when I spun in turn three right in front of him during practice. I was the rookie driver and he was the veteran, so his laughter was spiced with grumbles. Mine, with a little trepidation! A short time later I said goodbye to Los Angeles, and became a Wyoming state trooper. I lost touch with Tim and Tina. I will always be sorry for that. Ten years later, I learned of Tina's murder.

Today, there is a small memorial near the place where Tina was killed, and her name is emblazoned on the National Law Enforcement Memorial in Washington, D.C.

God bless, Tim.

Pink Volkswagons

Some time ago a list of questions was put to me from readers asking what really goes on behind my "Ray Bans." Cops wear Ray Bans.

Anyway, these were supposedly questions they would ask if there were a no holds barred "bull session" between cops and citizens.

One question was, "Is there a particular car we look for to stop, more than other types."

No. Blaming the car, whether it is a black Ferrari or a pink Volkswagen, is kind of like blaming the pot for lousy soup. Or, like blaming the teacher for an "F" when we don't turn in our homework. Or like blaming the beans we ate for … well …

All motor vehicles have one inescapable flaw in common. You can pay $250,000 for a Rolls Bentley, or $500 for you neighbor's "Hey…it runs" clunker. All of them are controlled by human beings, some of whom are just certain they won't get caught if they just "fudge" a bit and drive faster than the law allows. It makes no difference what color, what make or what model. None. If your pink Volkswagen or black Ferrari comes into my field of vision and you are doing something naughty, I will stop you and we will visit. There. Next question …

"Have you ever written a ticket which wasn't justified?"

Huh? Who … me? The answer is no. Well … almost no. Listen up, because I am about to admit something very few have ever believed they would hear from the mouth of a cop. Ready? Seat belt fastened?

"I AM HUMAN!" It feels so good to say that!

The truth is, *yes*, I have written some bogus paper. And I have stepped up to the plate and tattled on myself to the prosecutor each time, asking that the citation be dismissed. How can that be?

Well, for example, there have been occasions where a law has been changed in the legislature, and I (remember we are human) forgot. My mind just plain vapor locked. The result? A cite for an act no longer illegal. Or, I have noticed an external or electronic error message when I have checked my RADAR (something done after each RADAR citation). Then, I get that, "Oh NO! I coulda had a V-8!" look on my face, complete with a slap on the forehead. Usually, I mumble unbecoming expletives all over the patrol car, and then immediately issue a legal document called a "3M Stickymus Notemus," asking the court for the cite to be dismissed, and attach it to the original. This is usually followed by a telephone call to the court explaining why. Very embarrassing indeed. There. I admit it. Now, can we go to the next question?

"What was the best excuse you ever heard, and did it work?"

How's this? "My wife is … LOOK … *THE BABY IS COMING OUT!*"

Know what? After the five mile "lights and si-REEN" escort to the hospital, I helped as a baby was born on the gurney in the parking lot in Evanston, Wyoming. Somehow, I forgot to cite the proud, new daddy.

Don't let it get around. I got a reputation to maintain.

The Final Answer

Your police receive the most initial and ongoing training for two things. The legal justifications and edicts regarding the use of deadly force, and then the skillful and decisive application of it should it become necessary. Unfortunately, it is a real part of this job.

The use of deadly force is obviously the very last level of force there is. Using it ends it all. A life, and sometimes a career. The legal considerations and moral stigma it leaves on the officer usually result in his or her leaving the business. Even when completely exonerated of any wrongdoing and fully justified. The fact is, after its use, very few have a desire to return to the street. They try, but it is never the same. Never. As a comparison, it's like conquering a phobia. Once you do it the fear is gone. However, in police work, the fear is what keeps us alive. On our toes. On the edge.

You see, never knowing when something may happen, by necessity, keeps us ready to respond in a millisecond at the moment a threat is perceived. Missing it means death. It cannot happen.

Ironically, to accept the role of "Peace Officer" one must on the very first day of training accept the likelihood that a deadly attack will someday happen. And then we must resolve to be more deadly, more ruthless and more cold-blooded than the bad guy ever dreamed of. To absolutely win the fight. You see, it is not dramatic, romantic, or smooth and dignified. It is harsh, cold and emotionally crushing. There is no background music, no happy ending. Deadly force is ugly. In the instant-decision scenario faced ninety-nine percent of the time, the street officer must decide *immediately* to live or die. And then act instinctively with blinding speed. To do less is fatal.

Understand that, God forbid, one of us should find ourselves in that awful place, it was the violent felon who decided it would go this way, not us. The action we take is to stop the danger and end the violent intentions of a very bad person who, at that instant, wants to kill you or us.

Finally, I hope beyond words the day never comes, and someday I retire having never faced the foreboding scenario I have described here. Nevertheless, I am a realist and I know it very well might. Years ago I made my decision—my resolution. Then sometime later I became a husband. Then a father. Life changed and now ... well...

Each day the last thing I do as I walk out the door for work is kiss Mrs. Geeting and our two young men—at least when they're home. I look them straight in the eye and make sure they understand my love and devotion for them has no bounds and will live forever, no matter what might happen. Then I walk out to my patrol car to begin my tour of duty knowing in my heart I may have just said my last goodbye.

As I start the patrol car and drive off I pray in silence, asking for the blessings of good judgment and courage, quickness and, yes, precise skill, should this be the day. If it is—there is one absolute known by my family, and now by you.

I will win, or I will draw my last breath trying.

A Voice in the Night

One of the most common misconceptions about rural law enforcement like the Wyoming Highway Patrol is that we work alone. The truth is we are never alone. Not ever. It just looks that way.

While there is usually but one soul sitting in that patrol car, there is another always there. A voice in the night, always calculating, planning and sensing, right next to us. And while powerless to physically help, the unseeable one is always the first to know when things are going bad, or when help is needed. This unseen partner is the one who makes it all happen. The 911/police radio operator. The dispatcher. I want you to know about these men and women, as they are a full member of our batallion—not just our "right arm"—but our partner at every level.

They are every bit a part of your public safety force as are the folks in the flashy cars and snappy uniforms basking in all the glory. Without our dispatchers, getting people like me to respond to your need would be impossible by today's standards. And the acclaim they so richly deserve rarely comes their way because they are only heard, never seen. The truth is they have saved lives, including the lives of many cops. You should be proud they work for you. And thankful!

If they are good at this work, they are protected and revered by the cops they work with. If they lack the gift this profession demands, they don't last long. You see, this job requires the clerical skills of a secretary and the urgent compassion of a suicide hotline counselor. The technical expertise of a computer programmer, PBX operator and disk jockey, with a human touch at the end of the line; extracting critical information from a screaming victim in need of life saving help. They must be able to read a map within seconds and give detailed directions to a place they have never been. At any given moment they are keeping track of multiple officers. Some on traffic stops, some on building searches and others handling domestic disputes, armed suspects, neighborhood problems or bar fights—all at the same time! If you're thinking this is impossible, you're right.

Once, just for kicks and giggles, I tried to take a part of the Wyoming Highway Patrol Dispatcher entrance examination, wherein the applicant sits in front of a simulated radio console. On this console are buzzers, lights, buttons, switches, knobs, dials, pegs, hoops and slots. Then the phone rings and at the other end is a woman screaming very loudly, who needs … well … something! Your task is to listen and gather the information.

While that is going on a tape recorded voice gives orders like, "Put three green hoops on the red peg"… "Turn the green dial to four, and the yellow knob to letter Q." "Flip the five white switches to on, and the three red switches to off." "Put two red cards in slot number 7"…

This goes on and on, faster and faster. A good candidate will keep up with this nonsense for a minute or two. After fifteen seconds, I am embarrassed to say I got so mad I drew my gun and nearly put two rounds into that lousy, stinking tape player! Give me fast cars, gunfights and drunken brawls. But this? You gotta be kidding!

I have often wondered why, with all the stress of this work, anyone would do it? And finding no answer in all these years, I simply thank God that they do.

Scanner Freaks

Imagine this. You're laying there sleeping at oh, say 4:30 AM, all snuggled up in deep REM sleep, happily content as your brain quietly catalogues all of the input from the last day. Your room is cool and dark, the silence only slightly adulterated by the quiet and muffled snore of the family dog. All is well and as it should be.

Suddenly the dead quiet and dark silence of your bedroom is beaten and battered like a snare drum, as an abrupt and static-ridden police radio calls out "10-52," "10-51," "10-50" and a bunch of other "10" stuff. Then sirens are heard in the background as urgent police, fire or ambulance crews drive at breakneck speed screaming into their microphones to "10-9," "10-12," "10-18" and "10-78!"

If you're a regular guy or gal, you would shoot about three feet off the bed, grab your heart, turn off the alarm or maybe answer the phone. Completely confused for about two minutes until your heart could slow down, your mind could adjust and the panic could subside. But chances are you'd be up for the day. No way you go back to sleep. No way.

To a scanner freak this blaring pandemonium is a lullaby and only serves to perhaps affect a quiet little rollover, or at most, a quick trip to the bathroom before slipping back under the covers to continue their slumber. They usually don't even notice what was said.

Normally scanner freaks are harmless and find it oddly addictive to listen to the chatter, actually using the little device as you might use a softly playing radio or environmental noise player. You might like to sleep to the sound of a seashore or waterfall, but scanner freaks dig ten codes, screaming sirens and static.

These curious citizens like to listen because it can sometimes be exciting and, in fact, entertaining. Scanner freaks soon come to know many of "their" officers by first names, all of their call numbers, area assignments and even individual habits or vernacular. They know all of our sneaky little "codes" and tricks to try and fool them. They really get miffed when tactical teams sometimes scramble their radio.

Scanner freaks are regular people. Every once in a while some civilian will walk up to me in the store and say something like, " Man, that sure was a bad wreck last night out at Bitter Creek," or, "So ... how's Deputy Smith since his surgery?" Some of our most devoted listeners have even sent get well cards after an officer was injured. One guy even showed up at my doorstep with a pot of soup, after I'd been severely injured when I was hit at 75 mph by a tractor-trailer while I was parked on the side of the road giving another guy a ticket!

"Dad, there's a scumbag at the door!" My son had answered a quiet knock at the side porch. The "scumbag" as it turned out, was a well-known community recluse with long hair and a big beard who lived out in the desert, but was a certifiable scanner freak. He had heard me screaming for an ambulance the night I was injured and just wanted to see if I was okay or needed anything.

Good-natured and well-intended use of emergency scanners can provide a glimpse into our world, and can show you best the meaning behind one very popular description of police work ...

Ten hours of boredom punctuated by a few seconds of sheer terror!

Seven & Seven

His eyes told the story loud and clear. Tears flowed, relieving the pressure from the intense fear and confusion. All he wanted was his mommy and dad. He didn't care that his dad was drunk. He didn't care that his dad had just murdered a carload of teenagers. He just wanted his daddy.

This was one of the first fatal crashes I ever worked. I was twenty-six years old and a baby fresh rookie to the work of a state trooper. I only wish something had prepared me for this.

I tried everything to avoid talking to this child and having to deal with him. I faked the need for measurements to be taken when they had already been done. I acted rushed to inspect some far-off corner of the crime scene, when there was no need for me to go. When asked by a seemingly insensitive reporter what had happened, I snapped off something about being too busy, but that perhaps the little boy could help him out. When that same reporter started to walk over and do what I sarcastically suggested, he felt my sudden and firm grip on his skinny arm. The broken glass crunched under my boots. I was not happy.

"Is that his dad?" the reporter asked looking at the blood-soaked blanket on the ground. He winced as he tried to pull his arm away. Finally I let go as we put some distance between the boy and ourselves.

"Yes it is. He's dead, okay? So are four kids in that car," I whispered, glancing and nodding over to the wreckage of a Toyota Corolla draped in sheets as the Coroner waited to fill his bags. It was once a gift from the proud parents of an honor roll senior. Now, it was an ugly monument to her death, and that of three more perfectly hopeful and brilliant children. Before dawn two more would die. The killer's wife and her unborn little girl. Seven dead and a seven-year-old orphan. All for the love of booze. All for the kick of one of humanity's most addictive drugs. Alcohol.

Every ounce of my being yearned for a chance to hurt the person responsible for this. One of a cop's realities—this wanton hatred—with nowhere to put the anger other than to swallow hard and force back the burning bile in our throat. The bad guy in this case was dead. His boy, the only survivor of this crash, would soon become much more of a man than most men will ever be.

In the year his dad was taken, the two had gone to three baseball games, camped out for a week in the mountains and had laughed too many times to count—occasionally to the hysterical point of tears. They loved each other in a way only a child can love their dad—and that only a dad can love his child. And then it was over.

This is one of my war stories. It is real, and heartfelt.

As you read this there are hundreds of very lucky men and women in this country waking up with hangovers, perhaps in some jail cell, incarcerated for drunken driving. Somehow they managed to avoid a disastrous collision caused by their criminally selfish behavior.

They beat the odds. They will go about their lives, knowing no one has been hurt because of them. At least not yet. Unless stopped, they may try the gamble again.

For them, I offer this. Drinking and driving is no longer something society giggles about, shrugs off or quietly gives allowance for. Thankfully, in today's world, driving while intoxicated is not accepted and is an embarrassment bringing shame your families. Count your blessings, thank God for your luck, and walk away a winner.

Cash in your chips, and never again drive after drinking. Never.

Pretenders to the Throne

Recently I received an interesting letter from a reader with seemingly strong viewpoints as to the validity of police powers over the people of the United States of America. Without delving into too much detail, he held the view that the requirements of our constitution and many of our statutes were unconstitutional. He mentioned the seat belts and DWUI just to name a couple. In fact, this gentleman informed me that many of the appointed and elected officials of our country, including cops, were pretenders to the throne and should be arrested and prosecuted for treason. Although I would proudly give my life defending his right to express it, it was just his opinion. I hope he understands he could be wrong.

My opinion is that his opinion is emotionally based, and while ill conceived, is harmless unless he acts out this belief with willful disobedience or violence. One treads on dangerous and possibly felonious ground should one resist, interfere with, or physically strike a police officer performing their official, lawful duty. Understand that we as police officers cannot and do not consider a person's opinion of our legitimacy or the constitutionality of the law, when we need to arrest them because they disobeyed the law. It is only important that they "go with the flow" and let the system do its job.

Police officers (whether we are seen as "legit" or not) take a sworn oath, both verbally and in writing, to defend and protect both their state and United States constitutions, and to act upon any law or regulation they see violated. That is their promise to you and most of them take it as the solemn and momentous statement it is meant to be. Whether or not they as individual citizens personally agree with those laws or, fervently disagree with them as is sometimes the case, they can never let this enter into their actions or inactions. This character trait—the ability to set aside personal or emotional bias—is the reason backgrounds are checked thoroughly, neighbors are interviewed, work and credit history painstakingly verified and inspected. Finally, they must take and pass an intensive psychological screening test comprised of hundreds of questions and sit down for a face-to-face chat with a psychiatrist. All to assure they are of sound mind, honorable character, and ethically strong enough to see it through. Usually, this screening process works pretty well.

Indeed, your peace officers do actually sign a copy of the oath of office and it is a legally binding document. Willful reluctance, malfeasance or neglect of its promise, or omission of any duty described in it, is and *should be* cause for removal from office and, possibly, criminal prosecution.

The gentleman who wrote to me, quite obviously intelligent and well-read, had gone to painstaking lengths to extract and quote to me court findings and opinions seemingly bolstering his claims. However, as is unfortunately and frequently the case, he failed to look at the cases these rulings came from in their entirety and context.

All peace officers are legitimate and constitutionally authorized representatives of government, and all of us have made the exact same sworn promise before God to protect every citizen at all costs.

Even those who would rather we didn't.

A Valentine Promise

When each of my two sons were born, I wrote both of them their very first Valentine from their daddy. The magical tenderness I felt for them was far beyond anything I ever thought I could feel. Today they are as much a part of my life as the air I breath. A huge part of what I am.

Up until my boys came along, my life as a police officer did include children from time to time. Whether it was at the scene of a crash, domestic violence or arresting someone they were with for DWUI, I was somehow able to set aside their screams of sorrow and grief in a cold and clinical fashion. However, once I had kids of my own those days were gone forever.

Suddenly all children, no matter who they belonged to, became these complete little people deserving of my full care and my heartfelt compassion. Their safety in my role as a state trooper became, and remains, my highest priority.

I just said all of that to discuss child restraints. In a crash, this simple device, when of certified quality and being used correctly, can prevent massive injuries or the death of a child. It is that plain. It is that simple.

The true forces of a crash, even of relatively slow, residential speeds, are completely beyond belief. Even with a state trooper's hundreds of hours of advanced classroom training on crash investigations where I am constantly reminded of why I should have paid better attention in my high school algebra class, I am still amazed at the damage and human suffering caused by relatively minor crashes. I am further astonished that even when we point out the fragility of human beings in seat belt presentations to the public, it seems that only devastating pain and deformed dashboards convince the ever doubtful who claim safety restraints don't work.

In a fender bender of only fifteen miles per hour, an unrestrained three-year-old little person will fly through the interior of your car at twenty-two feet per second. That means if in the back seat, their tiny, unblemished, innocent little face will collide with the windshield in about a fourth of a second. The force will be more than enough to shatter their little neck and spine, or destroy every tiny facial bone. All because an adult—or should I say someone with a driver's license—was too busy, too selfish, or too ignorant to secure that little person properly. A safety seat will hold their little body and keep it still like no adult can.

My Valentine's Day message to our sons is private and someday (a wedding perhaps?) we will dig it from one of the many, many boxes of "SAVE" stuff in storage. Every mom and dad has a "SAVE" box. Okay—ten boxes! On that day I will no doubt shed a tear and feel like only a parent can—a paradox of heartache and joy—which comes on the day we realize our children have grown and reach for another's hand. On that sheet of paper will be a promise we made to them as infants to always protect them and shelter them from harm. A small part of that promise will have been accomplished using child restraints.

Please. If you can't listen to me, listen to your heart, listen to your doctor, listen to all who've ever had their heart broken by this needless tragedy. Use a child restraint!

Just Another Hero

Living among you is a bit of a legend. A man deserving of your respect, your gratitude and your pride.

His moment came back in 1981 when his duty found him south of Rock Springs, Wyoming, running toward what others can run from. Evil. Toward the danger, when good sense told him otherwise. You demand this of your government. Protection. That's why you pay your taxes.

A bad person had robbed a bank at gunpoint in Colorado and was making his escape through Wyoming. Easy, he thought. He would just slip through rural Wyoming where nothing—no one—would see him, and enjoy the fruits of his crime. Your hero—a Wyoming State Trooper—received a message to be on the lookout for this man. He did. And he found him.

As the two cars—the black and white and the suspect's car—passed on the lonely state highway before arrangements could be made for support, the bad guy abruptly stopped his car, forcing the trooper's hand. In a flash—mere milliseconds—the bad guy was out of his car and shooting at the trooper. Before he could react, the state trooper was shot. The first round came through the windshield, through his sunglasses and into the trooper's eye. His eye was destroyed by high velocity bullet fragments and glass. His reaction to duck for cover resulted in five more rounds plugged into his back, as the brazen gunman ran back to the patrol car and attempted to finish him off. He failed.

Bleeding now with a pulverized eye and five bullets in his body, he summoned his courage and an indescribable spiritual strength. He rose to his feet and, bleeding profusely from his face and back, shot back at the man who was now driving away, fearing the man would kill other brother officers now coming to help. With all that had happened to him, he hit the suspect through the back window and through the driver's seat with one .357 magnum round, piercing the suspects shoulder. Then he collapsed.

Shortly, his help started to arrive. He was soon in the arms of a friend—another state trooper who would have died protecting him. No one would hurt this man any more. A short foot pursuit with other officers soon resulted in the suspect's surrender. Ironically, an hour or so later the wounded state trooper and the man who would have killed him lay side by side in the emergency room of the same hospital. The doctor worked on the trooper first.

Today the assailant is in prison. He is visited often—by of all people—the man he shot. His victim has forgiven him, something I could not do. The victim is a better man than I am.

The state trooper is now a Deputy Sheriff in Sweetwater County, Wyoming. His name is Steve Watt. Now, you know more than his name.

Suspicious Minds

Being suspicious, or at least skeptical, is a quality essential to good police work. Most people like to give others the "benefit of doubt." We cannot. If we did that, many well-founded suspicions about shaky characters would just be shrugged off, allowing very bad people to get on with whatever lousy thing they were doing. You do not pay us to do this. You pay us to be suspicious of everyone and everything in your community until we are convinced all is well.

Sometimes that means questioning people, or at least eyeballing people as we patrol your neighborhoods. In Wyoming we have a luxury of small towns. In small towns, police can often get to know most of the activity on your street at any given time. We come to know who comes home or goes to work and when. Which cars and trucks belong where. Which kids are home alone, and where we have had domestic problems or neighbor disputes.

Have you ever been questioned by a police officer patrolling by? Has the officer asked where you live or what your address is? Chances are you were either at an odd place or there at an unusual time of day. You may take offense, but it's part of the job. Like a receipt for the taxes you pay. It is proof to you that that officer is protecting you and your neighborhood and checking on something unusual for you. You pay for that and you should feel good about getting your money's worth!

Imagine, for example, an officer patrolling your neighborhood at about 11:00 at night. He or she sees a figure of a person carrying a huge, heavy black sack out from behind your house and into the alley or street. Do you want that person stopped and questioned, or should we just extend the "benefit of doubt" and drive away assuming nothing is wrong? I mean ... it could just be YOU carrying out the trash! You pay us not to assume anything. We don't.

School yards and perimeters, shopping centers and business districts are some of the other areas of a community we watch very, very closely. During the school day, any pedestrians or occupied parked cars near schools are scrutinized very closely. We know how priceless your kids are. We have them too.

The night brings out some pretty odd ducks who can hide their activities in the darkness and avoid being seen. Our only tools here are insatiable curiosity and light—flashlights, floodlights and spotlights. With modern technology becoming more affordable, night vision equipment; portable and easily used by the street officer is available, but still not quite cheap enough to equip every patrol unit. Until then, please forgive and take comfort in the alley lights momentarily filling your dark homes with instant sunlight in the wee hours as we ensure your family a peaceful night—full of slumber, free of concern.

Finally, understand that in the history of modern day police work, society has seen a clear need for an inquisitive force empowered by the community to ask the questions and remove the bad guys who fail to follow the rules. Unfortunately, doing this occasionally means questioning innocent citizens who by mere chance happen to find themselves in an unusual place at an unusual time.

We know you're cool, but you pay us to verify it. That is what we do. Every time.

A Sacred Legacy

In the world of public safety and emergency services, we come to accept that sometimes we are taken for granted by the public we serve. Our knowledge and expertise remain largely unknown by the people we protect unless we are needed. This is not due to disrespect or ill will on their part, but simple ignorance and complacency brought on by a lifetime of peaceful bliss. Without any major trauma, fire, crisis, disaster or suffering from violent crime to remind them, our citizens never come to know all we can and do provide for them. For example ...

First Responders, Emergency Medical Technicians and Paramedics are some of the finest of humanity and true brothers and sisters in this family of ours—this family of man. Rarely do they get the recognition they deserve. Many of these heroic people were killed in the attacks and aftermath on September 11, 2001, right next to and in some cases in front of the police and fire personnel you have heard so much about. They were violently taken from society in an instant when the Trade Center collapsed. In their zeal to help, they ran into hell and into a sacred legacy.

Hundreds of thousands of these highly-trained medical professionals stand ready, willing and waiting, the instant they are called to hurry to your side and save your life. And understand this—most of them are paid absolutely nothing whatsoever for their work.

They seem to answer a calling. They put themselves through months and months of training at their own expense after work or on weekends, just to have the privilege of wading through the chaos and smoke to go directly to the aid of helpless victims. They somehow overlook the graphic ugliness and horrendous sights and smells all around them (not to mention the risk of injury, death, or a long agonizing battle with a fatal blood born disease contracted from a bloody victim), just for the chance to help. Those who volunteer respond from home, factories, farms and office buildings when their beeper goes off. The full-time few in larger metropolitan areas hold some of the most highly coveted jobs in emergency medical work— that of being paid for something they would do for free. How much are they paid? Far less than you might imagine, and much, much less, than they should be.

Another unsung but crucial element of emergency services is the Emergency Management Agencies and personnel. These are the people who provide the food, aid stations, warm shelters and guidance to citizens too frightened and unprepared to think of and then provide for their own basic needs.

In some communities there are well-staffed organizations with professional coordinators. In smaller communities there are only the churches, fraternal organizations and sometimes even school personnel—again—unpaid or compensated for being there and giving of hours, days and sometimes weeks of their time, not to mention money, food and simple emotional support to victims of natural or man-made disasters. And yes. The events of September 11, 2001, took some of these giving, selfless people as well.

The glory—that sacred legacy—is theirs too. Honoring all who still answer the call is our humble tribute. God bless.

Spring Time And Short Sleeve Shirts

All state troopers and many local cops celebrate April—not as the beginning of spring—but as the beginning of the seven month period we are permitted to wear short sleeve shirts AND NO TIE! Hot Dog!

While a small minority of my brethren like to wear long sleeves and a tie all the time, most cops hate them and jump for joy the second they become optional. 00:01, April 1—a moment truly anticipated. In truth, many are also permitted the option of a mock turtleneck in lieu of a tie, but it is almost as uncomfortable.

In addition to the short sleeved uniform, bugs on the windshield and a sunburn on the left forearm and left side of the face, there are many other signals to cops that summer is coming, with the frigid cold giving way to warmer temperatures—even if just for a few months. Department stores put the garden stuff out in the parking lot where a large portion is stolen, and decent people like you and me buy the rest so we can gleefully spread, sprinkle, whack, prune, mow, dust and plant. Cars and scooters are washed and waxed and driven across town, or across the country by happy motorists. Often way too fast.

Some with the power of the pen like those who wear those nice, comfortable, short sleeved uniforms are charged with catching these good but otherwise speedy people. We watch in amazement as hundreds upon hundreds of motorists, purposely and intentionally violate a law they know is vigorously enforced and seem willing to pay the three-digit fines and risk much higher insurance premiums. All for the thrill of spending more on gas, driving with the anxious eye on the mirror and dreading the impending short sleeved cop just over the next hill. Then when the inevitable happens, we meet on the side of the road and get to see the expression of stunned disbelief as we offer the news that a citation will be issued. We understand part of this is the realization that their worst worry came true, but it is still amazing to see.

Gee—can't you just give me a warning?

Chapter Three
Cops and Kids

Nice Bike

A child straddling a ten-speed bike far too big for him but obviously his—handed down from a bigger sibling I suppose—peddled awkwardly up to me yesterday. I was getting back in my "Bat-mobile" after filling my mongo mega-mug at the corner convenience store, and he at first gave a shy smile and a quiet, "Hi." I could tell he wanted to visit, but his manners and respect made him very reserved.

"Whasup little guy?" I said with a big smile to loosen things up.
"Nice bike."
"Yeah. Nice car. Is it fast?"
"Yep. She'll scream, but I try not to go that fast unless I have to. That a ten-speed?"
"Fifteen."
"Fifteen? WOW! Whatcha gonna do with all them gears?"
"I dunno." The young man laid his bike over and walked up to lean on my open window as I sat inside. He never once looked at me—but was mesmerized at all the gadgets, switches, dials and knobs, not to mention the three different microphones hanging on the dash.

Suddenly he fixed on my locked shotgun and asked, "That a shotgun?"

"Yep."

"Ever shoot anybody?"

"Nope. Don't want to either."

His eyes fixed on my dashboard. "What's this do?"

"That's my radar. It's how we catch speeders."

"What's the fastest you ever caught?"

"137." That one forced a glance with wide eyes directly at me.

"WOW!"

"How fast is your bike?"

He shrugged. "I dunno. What's that do?" he asked, ignoring my question and pointing to my overhead video console.

"Well, that's where I control my camcorder. I video tape stuff."

"Cool. Like wild Police Videos!"

"There you go. Like that."

"What are all those mics for?"

"Well, that one is my C.B. for talkin' to truckers. And this one is my public address speaker out there on the bumper. And this big one is my police radio."

"What's that for? Bad guys?" He gestured to my prisoner cage, reaching over to touch it. I nodded and waited for the next question.

"You wear a bulletproof vest?" He quickly glanced at my chest for the telltale bulges and just as quickly glanced back up, as though he wasn't supposed to look.

"I sure do, pal. I always wear it."

"Why?"

" 'Cause I got boys like you." He didn't get it. Then he smiled. He got it. "By the way, what's your name?"

"Joshua. But my friends call me J.C. How 'bout you?"

"I'm Jim. Okay, well, I better get to work, J.C. Enjoy that bike."

"See ya." He quickly started off, but then looked over his shoulder at me as he shakily peddled away. Then, with a huge grin he yelled, "Enjoy the car!"

Cops and Kids

Long ago, in the years of my young adulthood, I could not picture myself a dad. I didn't know how. It wasn't that I didn't like children, but more that I didn't understand them. I knew nothing of what made them tick.

Then I met and married my beautiful bride and, soon, Mrs. Geeting and I became parents. I have known no greater pleasure since. I became a different man.

As a police officer, one finds various occasions to contact and influence kids. In some cases we seem the heavy. In others the hero. A mystic surrounds us and, often, we are feared. The reason for this is clear to us, but seems to escape some parents.

While with their children in some public place who are perhaps antsy or misbehaving, some parents will see one of us nearby and say something like, "Look Billy, there's a cop. You keep it up and I'll have him take you to jail!" Or, "Officer, could you please arrest my kid? She's being a brat." It happens. A lot. And understand this—we hate it!

To have a fear of police might be understandable I guess; especially if a person has been in trouble or has been feeling guilty about something. However, to pass on this fear to your little people for no good reason is wrong and hurtful. A child comes to us full of God's love and a beautifully innocent trust. When they are brainwashed in this way they can grow up hating or fearing the police for absolutely no discernible reason. What a shame.

If you would like to assure your child grows to respect but not fear the police, there is a simple and very effective way to do it. It costs nothing and just takes a moment or two of your time.

The next time you see one of us, simply walk up with your little person and say hello. When this happens to me, I am thrilled at the chance to affect a child's outlook, and humanize myself by simply shaking hands, sharing a joke and a laugh with your child. As you introduce us to each other, you're telling your child he or she can trust us, and go to us when they need help or are in trouble. Most importantly, you tell them we are flesh and blood just like them, with a sense of humor and warmth. Let them wave at us as you drive past us on a trip. Bring them by your local police station and get a tour. In short, remove that mystic and give them a friend they will have for the rest of their lives. Someone they know is on their side.

As a police writer I am honored to know hundreds of cops all over the United States. I can attest that each one of them would die for your child without hesitation.

All we ask in return are their big smiles, high fives, and parents who understand this.

God Whispered

Is the reason we do this cop thing the glory and fame? I think not. There is no glory in a drunk puking on your shoes. No esteem from the victims at blood-soaked crime scenes, and no fame forty-five miles away from the nearest reporter or television camera out on some cold, lonely, two-lane road at four in the morning. As you measure and photo everything that applies, there is no audience, applause or cheers, other than some mangy coyote just beyond the flood of your headlamps, watching you curiously but not brave enough to venture closer. He could care less if your investigation is thorough and professional, and won't ever tell if you cut corners to get home out of the cold, driving wind a few minutes sooner.

Is it the great pay and perks? Hardly. The prestige and standing? You would be amazed. Take us out of uniform and no one knows us. Those of you who have met me know I am tall—6'10". Yet, still, occasionally when someone does recognize my name or me, as I produce ID and a credit card to write a check, they'll say something like, "Gee, I didn't recognize you out of uniform!" I must look like every other 6'10" customer they see!

I suppose the flashy car and snappy wool uniform is neat to younger men and women on the job, but as you get mellow and worldly with age you come to envy the people you see everyday who get to work in comfy, cool cotton jeans, no tie and hey—get this—short or long sleeves any time they choose! They don't have to bother constantly polishing their shoes, gun belt, brass or gold attachments, buckles, badges and bars. They can quietly slip into a coffee shop during a storm, and not have a line leading up to their table ten deep with less than happy travelers asking why the road is closed, when it will open, and just how the weather is in Kansas City and what will it be like tomorrow in Denver.

None of the romantic myths of police work come true, as you quietly but quickly remove a bloody uniform and place it in a plastic bag before your children see it. The background music doesn't play when you shower for thirty minutes at the end of watch until the water has run ice cold trying to wash away the filth and pain you've seen all day. Still, something keeps you going.

Recently, after I had just cleared from what was probably my 100th fatal traffic crash investigation near Point of Rocks, I accelerated away, set the cruise control, and thought about the reports I would be writing all day. I had been contemplating early retirement, and it had been these kinds of frustrating cases where some preventable thing had again killed someone on my highway—which made me question why I still did this job.

Cruising at 60 MPH in the right lane, I watched in my mirror as a brand new minivan slowly crept up to pass me. As the apprehensive driver eased by, both he and his wife stared straight ahead and seemed afraid to look over at me. Just then, three of the brightest little faces I had ever seen strained against their seat belts and looked over at me from the back seat. Smiling big smiles, they outwardly and intensely waved and waved and waved, as if terribly worried I would not see them. I was down, but I smiled and waved back at the kids, which of course brought out even bigger grins and giggles. I had made their day, and God had whispered a reminder.

I heard Him.

Again and Again

It had been an uneventful night, and as the trooper pulled into his driveway to end his shift the call came in. A one car rollover just five miles away. Multiple injuries, possible fatality. Adrenaline poured into his veins, his heart raced, and he accelerated toward the scene.

He was the first on the scene and was ten minutes ahead of the ambulance. As he stepped from his patrol car, what this trooper saw through all the broken glass, blankets, soda cans, potato chip bags, shoes and clothing, evoked an involuntary whisper, "Oh God. Oh no."

Through it all, in the eerie light of his spotlight, inside the twisted and ominous wreckage of what used to be a minivan, children's toys were strewn about everywhere. But the van was empty.

He found mom and dad right away. Both were quite obviously and graphically dead. Didn't believe in seat belts, apparently. It was obvious to the trooper that kids belonged to this couple but were not with the wreckage. The trooper panicked, fearing what he was sure to find.

Finally, in his flashlight beam some fifty feet from the car were the two little boys. One about eighteen months, the other about three-years old. Somehow, the two had been thrown and had landed within two or three feet of one another.

The little one had died instantly, but other than a trickle of blood from his ear he looked okay.

The trooper gasped as he knelt down and noticed the blue "feetie" pajamas on the dead child. His own baby had a pair just like them. Then he looked over at the second; the three-year-old. The little boy was alert and even forced a very frightened little smile. However, it could not hide his pain.

"Hi policeman, Oscar is scared. I have a bad tummy ache." The boy cried as he held on tightly to Oscar the Grouch. His appearance and symptoms were grave.

"How ya doin', little buddy?" said the trooper, fighting his breaking heart to return the smile. He knew the boy was dying, and lay down beside him, holding him tightly.

The medics arrived and loaded the youngster into the ambulance. The trooper looked down and saw that the youngster had dropped his Oscar the Grouch. He grabbed it and looked up to stop the ambulance, but it sped away. He walked over to his patrol car and tossed it in. He knew he had to hurry!

An hour later, after hastily getting through his investigation, he was standing in the doorway of the emergency room. A clipboard in one hand; a green fuzzy toy in the other. His uniform was soiled with sweat, dirt and blood. His face bore the grimace of recent, intense concentration.

The trooper walked over to the closed curtain of the examination bed. He flung the curtain open just in time to see the doctor pull a sheet over the beautiful, unharmed and peaceful face of the little boy. There was nothing to do but listen to the deafening silence. And once again witness complete waste. Something he had done again and again.

The trooper reached down with a filthy and callused hand, and stroked the boy's soft hair. Bending down, he whispered something in the boy's ear, gently tucked in Oscar and walked out of the hospital without a word. He drove home, called in sick, and walked into the bathroom ...

Can't Say Enough about my Kids

A few days ago I presented a bicycle safety program to the kids of my local school and, as always, completely enjoyed the company of we cop's biggest fans—the little people. The older kids were there too, but most of them have known me since they were in diapers and they don't seem too impressed anymore with my silly jokes and goofy faces, because they have all seen me every year. They don't ask me stuff about catchin' bad guys either, because to them I'm just a classmate's dad and a neighbor who lives down the street. And that's just the way I like it.

I simply can't say enough about "my kids." I have talked about the special relationship between cops and kids before and by gosh here I go again! With school soon to be over kids will be running around side streets, sidewalks and other places you'll never expect them, dropping out of trees and bringing home bugs and frogs to show us, so it's time to mention extra caution in residential areas.

Some of the most horrific crashes I have seen have been in quiet, tree-lined neighborhoods. It seems these quiet and familiar surroundings can lull us into a feeling of complete safety, when the reality is a car is huge and deadly whenever and WHEREVER it is moving.

Take extra time when backing from a driveway and triple-check underneath and behind your car before you start it, after you start it, and before you move. More than once I have had my heart broken as I responded to a fatality in somebody's driveway where a toddler was crushed as they played behind or underneath a car or truck. Pickups with high lift kits are a favorite for my little friends to build forts and play pretend games, with all the neat frame rails and axle housings. One case which still haunts me today involved a three-year-old little boy who was playing under his dad's pickup and dad was late for work. I will spare you the details, but a simple look would have prevented this life-changing tragedy. And as hard as I tried, sharing this man's grief was impossible to avoid.

A simple tap of your horn a couple of times to warn that little squirt you can't see as he races up the sidewalk behind the neighbor's shrubs will tell him you're backing out. Then back out VERY SLOWLY, looking repeatedly as you move, and be prepared to stop instantly—because little people are amazingly fast and agile.

Finally, let's talk about speed. Always remember the posted speed limit for residential areas is the absolute maximum, and you will not vaporize, turn to granite or be publicly ridiculed if you drive slower. If ten miles per hour feels too slow, try something. Run as fast as you can with your eyes closed into a brick wall. That's about five miles per hour. And it hurts!

No cop on God's earth will ever stop you for driving too slowly in a residential neighborhood. However, every cop I know will hammer you for exceeding this limit. I guarantee this. This is one speeding ticket I feel proud to hand out. If it ruins your day, so much the better. The youngster you endanger may be mine. Or yours.

And if you ever do get a ticket for impeding traffic in a residential zone, give it to me. I will shake your hand, thank you, and then I will pay it.

Her Last Breath

It's been many years now, but I remember her. Her look, her beauty and her innocence. One moment she was a five-year-old child with dolls and coloring books, the next a helpless victim struggling for her last breath. The sound of her little lungs trying so hard one last time to fill with life-giving oxygen, and then surrendering to her death will haunt me forever. It is one of those so very few moments even the most hard-cased on the job are powerless to stop. This one slipped past my crust. This one got to me.

Probably more heartbreaking than the sight of her unused car seat laying on the ground some 100 feet from the crashed car she was in, and more devastating than her dead mother laying within reach, were her dad and brother, both alive, and witness to what they had lost. Dad had a broken arm, but the little boy, surprisingly, was spared much injury. I don't know where they are now; I don't even remember their names. But their faces and their screams of pain and grief are mine to keep forever.

I was given this call as a one-car rollover; our most common crash in Wyoming. As I surveyed the scene, I saw she was still alive. I knelt down next to her in the sagebrush, and heard the unmistakable sound of her lungs filling with blood, trying to draw a breath. Her little face was unharmed. I held her hand, and in a few seconds it was over. It was then that I looked up and saw her father, sobbing at the side of his wife.

He looked over at me, and he knew. He asked; but his eyes told me he knew. His wife, and now his precious daughter, were gone.

Then his little boy looked down at his sister. Confused, frightened and hurting, he asked the obvious question. "Is my sister okay?"

As he sat down next to me, "G.I. Joe" in hand, I asked him to lay down and not to move until an EMT could look at him. Again he asked about his sister.

There is never a smooth or comfortable way to give this answer, but I would not lie or mislead him. Just as I was struggling for the right words, the boy's father sat down in the dirt next to him. With his good arm, he reached around and held his son, sobbing aloud. Then he told him the simple truth as gently as he could. The horror in this boy's eyes was overwhelming. My vision blurred and my throat swelled shut. I had to get up and walk away. Thankfully the EMT's had just arrived and they took over.

I later found out the boy and dad were buckled in, but that briefly—for just a few seconds—these well-meaning and loving parents had let their little girl out of her car seat to stretch and move around a bit. She had been complaining of being stiff. Mom had unbuckled just long enough to do it. Then, at that instant, they had a sudden tire failure. A blowout. They lost control and overturned, flipping many times like a toy in the interstate median. Dad had been driving.

With crushing shame in his eyes and voice, he told me they had been in a hurry. In a hurry, he said, to get to Disneyland.

Please … don't hurry. Take breaks. Don't be this man.

Nighttime Magic

Curfew. Society's version of Cinderella's pumpkin. And depending usually on the age of who you might ask, it is either a way to harass kids, or a way to keep them home and safe. Either way, kids hate it and, unfortunately, some defy it. Not a good idea.

The hours of curfew vary from town to town, state to state. Some change with the seasons, some with the days of the week. I remember when growing up in Los Angeles, at ten o'clock every weekday evening the TV announcer would interrupt whatever commercial was on and say, "It's ten o'clock ... do you know where your kids are?" My folks did. They always did. We were sitting right there in the family room munching on popcorn watching "All in the Family" or "Adam-12" (Dad was a cop, too), or in bed, or doing homework, or working on some project. But, yes, they knew EXACTLY where we were.

One of the biggest problems with a curfew is hormones! No, not the, "Hey, Baby, what's YOUR name?" kind, but the kind that start to wake teenagers up like a tall cup of 200 proof Colombian coffee just as the rest of mankind is getting tired. The "Nighttime is the Rightime" is more than a phrase in a song. For teens, it is as natural as their need for Oxy-5 and cheesburgers. Imagine being locked inside at the time of day you feel the most alive and energized. It's a raw deal! I remember I hated it, too. Not that I had somewhere to go, but that I couldn't go!

All I can tell our fantastic Sweetwater County teenagers out there is "cowboy up" and face the music. Just accept this protection and relish your youth. Don't rush the nightlife. It'll be there when you're ready, and with it a small collection of very bad, very unfriendly people who, like you, call the night their time as well. When the moon comes out, so do the wackos. Trust me on this one. You DO NOT need or want them in your life. I don't either, but it's my job to deal with them. I have to be out there. You don't.

Drunk drivers are lurking around every turn, just a blown red light or crossed centerline away from you. Temptations, and the pressures of fitting in, are high and sometimes impossible to avoid. Cruising seems cool, but understand you are but a whisper from crashing or hurting each other. Not because you want to, but because anyone driving a car excited about scoping things out and looking good, can sometimes miss a pedestrian, or warning, or hazard on the roadway.

Bottom line? All of us in law enforcement are enforcing the curfew locally, so my advice would be to use all of that God-given energy and stay home where it's safe and warm. Ask your parents about their day, or read, or get to know your kid sister, or pester your big brother, or build a model. Or, write a book—like me!

Yellow Limousines

Seems like just a couple days ago school was out and it was time to play. As of this very day our kids are back at the books, their teachers eager to shape young minds once again and, yes indeed; those great big yellow limos are on the job. Now there's a challenge for you…try driving a school bus! Think you have what it takes?

Okay, here's your challenge. Go ahead and get your Commercial Driver's License; a pretty tough test; both a written and a practical skill course. Obey to the letter every single traffic law—all of them, without so much as the hint of error or confusion, as there is no fudge factor—not even two miles over the limit. One slip and you will face severe criticism from every facet of oversight; your employer, parents, law enforcement and the kids themselves. Calmly accept this enormous responsibility. With the skill of a pro, drive this five-ton limousine in wind, snow, rain and icy roads so slick the result is quadrupled in effect and feel. Be passed and ignored by impatient commuters, even when your red lights are flashing for all they're worth. Be precisely on time at a dozen different stops. Greet five dozen happy little faces as though they are the most important person on your bus, and know with all certainty you and you alone are responsible for the lives of fifty or sixty kids; their safety and their welfare.

Do all of this for a level of pay not nearly worthy of your skill and dedication. Work a split shift and be on call for special events and field trips. Keep order and discipline behind you, while absolutely never taking your eye off the road in front of you.

If you are still interested, or you are currently on the job, this state trooper wants you to know I salute and tip my hat to each of you. Every parent who ever stood for the first time with a priceless little boy or girl waiting for their very first bus ride to kindergarten or first grade held a fear and trepidation deep within their heart, and silently whispered a prayer for a friendly, skilled and vigilant professional behind the wheel. Any parent will agree; to give up our little ones to a complete stranger would be absurd in any other circumstance, and every instinct in our souls tells us not to do it ... not to give up our precious cargo to you.

Nevertheless, the time comes as you pull up to the curb and, hopefully, a warm smile and a gracious, good-natured person will greet both our children and us. Understand, for that one moment—that one moment in time—you face a parent's judgment; and you are the most powerful and trusted human being on the face of the earth. And so you are; each and every day you protect our children with both your skill and your love.

A Chance to Make a Friend

There are places a police officer spends time which are usually off limits to the public—at least under normal circumstances. The squad room is one. The communications center is another.

Also normally off limits is the department shooting range. Recently, the Police Department was gracious enough to allow the local division troopers access and use of their basement range for our monthly firearms training. So, imagine my surprise when after I'd shot up the "ten ring" in my target, and had just finished reloading my duty ammunition into my magazines and sidearm, I looked up and saw about eight or nine happy little faces.

They were standing just outside of the range, wide-eyed and curious, along with about a half-dozen grownup "regular" people. It took about two seconds to realize this was some type of a field trip, and that these were probably preschool boys and girls. Of course, I just had to act the fool. I never miss a chance!

"Wow! Are you guys new POLICE OFFICERS?" I shouted to them all as a group. Most were a little shy, but one spry and gregarious little girl looked up at me with complete and utter pity, and answered, "No, silly, we're KIDS!"

"You are? You're kids? Well, gee—I thought you were police officers!" I rolled my eyes in an exaggerated self-effacing manner, bringing out a few more nervous giggles.

Just then I saw a couple of them looking at my "paper man," as they called it, the target we use which is actually a life-size photograph of a mean looking bad guy pointing a gun back at us. Soon one of our troopers stepped up to the firing line in the next room. While the firing line is secure and behind a wall of windows allowing for safe watching, it can still be quite loud.

"Everybody plug your ears!" said another officer to the kids.

"Like THIS!" I said, and stuck my fingers into mine. All of them did, giggled more, and watched with the innocent amazement only a child's face can portray as the trooper blasted away at his own "paper man."

Soon after this chance encounter, I received a note from the grandmother of one of the teachers there that day, who happened to be a retired WHP administrative assistant. She said the kids had a great time! She understood that I have even more fun than the kids do!

I have written before of the very special understanding and relationship between the police and the little people we protect. We learn that no affection is as genuine and unadulterated as the hugs, "high fives" and laughter of the little people we meet on the job.

These moments with kids give us the opportunity to be a friend and they are priceless. Unfortunately, they are also quite fleeting. For just a few short moments in the life of a little person, we as police officers can do more than just be the clown, look like a dork and get a few giggles. We can actually set kinship into the quickly drying mortar of their foundation, which will last them for the rest of their lives. We can choose to make this happen, or we can be too cool and miss it.

I choose to be the clown. To look like a dork and, oh my, get LOTS of giggles!

The Making of a Veteran

Horrendous motor vehicle crashes and the experience of investigating them are a regular task of the veteran police officer. Until this experience has occurred, complete with human tragedy and heartache, there is a huge void in the officer's resume. But sadly, the officer won't have to wait long. It will happen. When it does the officer will learn valuable lessons, for to come upon the scene of a crash as the one in charge can be overwhelming, emotional and extremely busy.

First, we must be the *objective* and distant collector of evidence, looking past the sometimes horrific scene before our eyes, collecting only those objects, observations, statements and markings which tell the story all want to know—what happened?

We must be the masterful crime scene photographer, hurrying to get the shot before curious fellow cops and onlookers move or touch objects crucial to the case, or before ambulance, fire and other emergency vehicles drive over critical markings in the dirt, or park upon some critical piece of the puzzle.

We must be skilled interviewers; taking statements, sifting through the spurious and less applicable mutterings of people who at first "*saw everything*," and then later, with painstaking and skillful questioning, come to realize they saw only the aftermath or heard the noise and *then* looked, not seeing at all what they thought they had.

In case of death we are criminal investigators, deciding if a homicide has led to this tragedy, or innocent human error. Sometimes the line between them is very blurry, and bringing it into focus will be our primary responsibility. People will be waiting to hear.

There are often other considerations which can take the skills of the clergy, but they are rarely on scene. At these times the police officer must fill that role as well, when simple human kindness, a warm touch, and quiet calm are all that is needed. This is not in the academy textbooks—this cannot be taught. The following is a real-life example ...

Two doctors and several EMT's were gathered around a gurney frantically working as hard as they could on one of two brothers involved in a crash. The doctors shouted out orders for supplies and tests, while the nurses and EMTs frantically applied their skills with a detached compassion. This was a six-year-old boy. Lying next to him, separated only by a thin curtain, was a young man of nine, now suddenly so much older. The police officer, a rookie of six months, stopped and sat down on a stool next to him. Together, the two could hear the others working on his sibling.

"That's my little brother over there. I love him," the boy said with a quivering voice to the probationary officer. "Do you think he's gonna go to heaven now?" The young man knew it was very serious, and began to cry.

The officer placed one hand on his little forehead, told him to relax, and to close his eyes. Together, they put out a wish to God and she held his hand until he fell asleep. It took almost an hour. Two weeks later, a mom and two bruised but happy little boys left the hospital. They would be okay.

And a rookie police officer became a veteran.

Some Kids I Will Never Meet

The other day I had the humbling experience of attending County Spelling Bee for sixth through eight graders. Among the finalists, my own son stood tall, brilliant and stunningly handsome, a chip off the, well, anyway ...

The first round was just for practice and included the word *POTATOES*. I leaned over to the professionally dressed woman who happened to be sitting next to me and whispered, "Well at least they got *that* one out of the way!" She came back with a comment herself and we shared a quiet moment of levity about vice-presidents and tubers—cut abruptly short by the teacher at the door—another professional woman with a no-nonsense look that made it clear she would bounce us right out of the room if we kept it up.

It became clear to me by her attentive mannerisms that the woman next to me was in some way attached to some of these children—a teacher—or perhaps a parent. A bit later, at round six or so, she asked if I had a youngster in the finals and I introduced her to the back of my son's head, "That's him in seat #3. That's *my* boy!" When

I mentioned his name, my new friend spun in her chair and introduced herself, "Well, you're the guy who lives with Mrs. Geeting!"

She stuck out her hand and I completed a firm handshake. I had just become friends with a teacher at Westridge Elementary School—and according to Mrs. Geeting I was right in my assessment. She was indeed every bit the professional I thought she was—a well-respected and veteran educator.

The two of us watched and shared a pride in these brilliant little people—she as one who perhaps had a small role in their success, and I as one of the many parents sitting there with the same claim. Both of us never quite certain if our contributions had much effect on the success of our children, but nevertheless spending hours upon hours with them in hopes of small moments like these. Just when Mrs. Myers and I were feeling pretty good about things, along came rounds eleven and twelve, with words dug up from the depths of some sadistic librarian's treasure chest—words with hair on 'em!

Words like *magnanimous, conscientious, luminescent* and *coefficient* caused a few struggles, but to my amazement most of the kids hung on by their fingernails. Finally, the time came to thin the crowd.

Words like *rutabaga, rubicund, Rosella* and *ruthenium* reared their ugly syllables, eliminating all but one—one youngster who should be very, very proud of herself. As for me? I was so amazed I can't even remember her final word!

As a cop in a very public role, it is very refreshing to quietly blend into the background and be an anonymous parent like everyone else. To watch a group of brilliant youngsters I will probably never meet in an official capacity. To watch a group of winners striving for academic excellence, instead a group of delinquents tagging a wall. And to shake the hand of a career educator and share a laugh in common—a moment of trepidation—as the bouncer looked our way.

On that day I wasn't a cop. Just a dad and citizen, so proud of all these kids.

Bells, Books and Busses

Two things happen in the fall—gardeners fear an early frost, and little people, fresh with several inches of new growth, brand new clothes, backpacks and tennis shoes strut off to get educated. With new classes, new kids and new teachers, the beginning of a new school year is both an exciting and a nervous time for children. And parents. And teachers.

I remember not too long ago, watching as my little boys walked off to school. We were fortunate and lived close by, so I watched every step they took for two blocks until they walked into the building. When a cop is also a parent it can be troublesome. Our knowledge of bad people just lurking out there waiting to steal or harm children is perceived intensely. We can lose sight of the comparative safety of the community and neighbors who care. But that's another story.

Anyway, get ready. Here come the yellow trucks full of little faces and smiles. All of us need to be sharply focused on the roads near school yards during the school year. School buses will be full of precious and irreplaceable cargo, and while passing one with red lights flashing will introduce you to me, it is more than the ticket. It is a selfish act and needlessly risks the lives of dozens of children. Those red lights tell you little people are running in and around that bus. And that big people like me are quite likely watching you.

A school bus is the safest means of transportation for children to and from school for many reasons. While the drivers have rules of conduct to maintain order and safety, it is always a good idea to visit with your children as the school year begins to remind them that you fully expect them to behave on the bus just like in a classroom. Ever been in a minivan full of out of control and shouting children? Can you imagine forty kids yelling along with the noise of the bus? Our bus drivers are far too valuable not to back them completely in their efforts.

As you drive through the immediate vicinity of a school, please understand that the potential for disaster is extreme. You see, during the time children are arriving or leaving, the last thing they are thinking of as they laugh and visit with friends is the traffic passing by. They are but a step or two away from you, and at a speed of twenty mph disaster is there just waiting for an opportunity.

If you are picking up your kids, remember not to get too distracted as they tell you of the adventures in their day. At the beginning of the school year they will be full to the brim with new names, new friends and new teachers. And they will want to share it all with you as you drive. Listen, but drive carefully.

A Good Cop and an Ice Cream Sundae

One tough situation faced by law enforcement is when a mom or dad in the company of a child commits a crime and needs to go to jail. And, of course, no other adult guardian for this child lives within 200 miles and something must be done to care for the child. For no fault of their own these small children must be taken from that one parent, and thrust into the care of a complete stranger. To say the least, it can be very traumatic to watch your mom or dad getting arrested, then even more damaging to be thrust into the arms of someone you don't know!

It happens—quite often. Recently, a rookie trooper I work with was put into an odd position with a young child in this same spot. How the trooper handled it was the best part of police work—helping the small and assuring the frightened. It went like this...

Another trooper had arrested this boy's father for drunk driving. With no one to call locally, the boy would have to be taken to the county juvenile custody center until his mom could arrive the next day. This eleven-year-old would have to spend the night in custody—there was no other way.

As soon as the rookie trooper arrived, he looked into the boy's frightened eyes and felt the agony we all do for children in fear and confusion. All the trooper had to do was transport this boy to juvenile hall. He didn't have to feel or care or smile. But he did all three.

With his completely natural comfort and confidence, Trooper Jim Gates smiled at the little boy. His compassion was genuine. His instinct was perfect.

"When's the last time you ate?" Gates asked, smiling wide and true.

The boy was shy. "I had breakfast." It was now 8:00 PM.

"Could you eat a burger or something?" asked the trooper without hesitation. If he bought dinner, the state would not reimburse him.

"No thank you, sir."

"Aw *c'mon!* How about an ice cream sundae?"

That did it. The shy boy slowly looked up and a small grin came over him. "Yeah! I could eat some *ice cream!*"

With that, they were off to a popular drive-through window. A good kid, a good cop and two ice cream sundaes to go.

Fun and Games Aren't

Will somebody tell me the thinking behind "Hood Surfing"? Geemonee Christmas!

I remember feeling ten-foot-tall and bulletproof as a young adult. I do indeed. But this one? This is something I didn't try. Never even thought of it. Last time I checked the Driver's Ed curriculum, they were still teaching that everyone should be *inside* the car and wearing safety belts—not putting their "knees in the breeze" on car bumpers and hoods. Am I right?

Listen. Asphalt and hard, packed dirt allow no room for horseplay, but do allow for a fun and safe afternoon cruise with a lot of common sense. And while you are free from the reins of the adults in your life for awhile when given the keys to the car, it will take only an instant of this nonsense to end it all. You may become one of the players in a very deadly game. The one who loses.

Families will fall to their knees in horrific disbelief that something so stupidly tragic could happen to their child, when a guy dressed like me has to tell them about your deadly game. Will it be your family?

And hey, if you were driving that car and too smart to be the "surfer" spinning slowly around the parking lot, guess what? You may end up taking a ride in a si-*reeen* car yourself, enroute to the worst nightmare of your young life. A life-changing, never ending stigma. A criminal negligence or reckless driving conviction if you are lucky. Vehicular homicide if the worst should happen. Yours to keep. Forever.

The truth is this: Inexperienced drivers and young passengers may feel infallible and made of steel. Over a career spanning two decades, having seen the torn flesh and bloody pulp which were once brilliant high school seniors or younger, I can assure you they, and you, bleed and hurt and scream just like everyone else. Your body is so fragile its life can be snuffed instantly at a wrong turn; a sudden crash.

The odds are against you already, without ignorant stunts like hood surfing. There are no "games" in cars. Ever.

Drive safe. Be good. Don't be stupid.

Love, Edward

One day many moons ago I was giving a presentation to a group of kindergartners. I sat on the floor with them and we talked of bad guys and si-REEN cars! Many wanted to know if I ever shot anyone and if I had ever been shot. As we all sat in a half circle on the floor, my eyes kept coming back to one little boy in the back row. He was very quiet, yet intensely staring at something on my shirt. I couldn't help worrying if I had dribbled some coffee on the spot he was fixed on, or if some other goober was besmirching my clean and snappy uniform.

With children this young, teachers will tell you "questions" tend to become "stories" and presenters can quickly lose control of everything. They will be deluged with, "One time there was this guy...." stories, fresh from the vivid imaginations of their open and curious five-year-old minds. As a veteran of losing such control, my schoolteacher bride has since taught me well, but there is one situation that comes up for which a ready answer does not exist.

"I have time for one more question," I said, looking directly at the quiet, young man, hoping to solve the mystery of my shirt. Without a word this young man stood up, and walked around the group until he stood next to me. Then, with an innocent hand, he simply reached out and touched the telltale slight bulge in my shirt where my ballistic vest pushed out my shirt.

"What's that?" he asked, sitting back down right next to me. The name on his shirt said, "Edward."

"Well ..." I thought hard how to answer Edward, but in the end I just did what I always end up doing with children. I simply told the truth. "That, is a bulletproof vest. Police officers wear them in case a bad guy tries to hurt us. It catches the bullets we can't duck."

"What if he shoots you in the head?" His blunt, straightforward retort and direct eye contact completely disarmed me. He wanted an answer, and he wanted it right now. The classroom fell silent.

"Well ..." I stammered for an answer the kids could understand, but again, as I sat there surrounded by these bright and supportive little people, I simply and quietly explained the reality.

"Well Edward, police officers are very special and brave people. They knew when they chose this life they made a very special promise to protect all of you no matter what. They will run into a house of fire, and will jump into a raging river to save your life. Because to a police officer, your life is more important and precious than their own. If you are in trouble and need their help, police officers will stop everything they are doing and run as fast as they can to fight for you. And, if they have to, to die for you. And so, Edward, I would probably get to go to heaven, because God likes police officers who protect little boys and girls."

Three days later, in my mail, I received a package of nine, hand-made crayon-colored thank you cards. One of them said, "Thank you for protecting us. And for wearing your bulletproof vest. And watch out for bad guys."

It was signed, "Love, Edward."

Chapter Four
Random Thoughts and Daydreams

An Intimidating Friend

Seldom at a loss for words, I found myself stopped cold when Dale Earnhardt ran his final race. As I sat dumbfounded just like tens of millions of others, Mrs. Geeting and I waited to hear if Dale was okay. It was later, as I drove in my patrol car (also black, albeit a Ford), when I heard by cell phone from a very tearful Mrs. Geeting that he was gone. She and I had watched and cheered for twenty years, as "Ironhead" did things with a race car that only a few before him had ever done.

Wait a minute you say? This is a book on law enforcement! Why am I discussing Dale Earnhardt? Read on ...

A well-known fact by the police across this country is that "The Intimidator" was a long-time, firm booster of law enforcement. A North Carolina State Trooper escorted Terry Earnhardt throughout her husband's memorial service. Many times Dale would hitch a ride with the state patrol in whichever state the race was that week, and with a trooper at his side the two would spot very conscienscious and careful drivers and stop them. One of them would approach the driver. But instead of the state trooper walking up to the driver, it would be a huge mustache in a ball cap wearing a big smile. Dale Earnhardt himself would be standing at their door, handing them a couple of his complimentary full pit-pass tickets.

Dale Earnhardt's charitable donations were in the millions, but the most memorable to regular people like you and me were these small but extremely powerful gestures by a guy who, to the die-hard long-standing fan of NASCAR, was up on the very, very tippy-top of the mountain, with only a handful of other guys in their sport. He, like those others, had started out at a small local track like Sweetwater County's Thunderdome, and ran a sportsman home built stock car while working and paying for it as a mechanic. He had nothing else given to him, other than mechanical knowledge passed on by his daddy—just as you and I might do for our kids.

Like other NASCAR icons he didn't "demand" more money, he raced for it. He didn't use drugs in any form. He set an example for all to see; that with aggressive hard work, tenacity and honest values, success is there for the taking.

As a lifetime Richard Petty guy, it has been tough for me to admit that "The King of NASCAR" had a modern day equal in Earnhardt, but he did. I always did acknowledge that truth. However, Petty's time was so different from present day, their two records just can't be compared. Both shared the most Winston Cup crowns, with seven apiece. Both were simply incredible drivers.

As a police officer, I hate to see such a good and decent human being of this caliber taken away from the young people I care so much about. Our kids. Children desperately need this kind of hero (to counter the ones who kill people, or sing about it), and such a loss brings on an overwhelming feeling of defeat.

For now, we all go on with a memory of a hero—or just a dad and husband watching unselfishly with certain joy and pride as his son Dale Jr., and good friend Michael Waltrip approached the finish line. Just like he had planned.

A cop's heroes are very, very few. Dale Earnhardt was among mine.

Cab Lizards

Many times I have been asked to address what seems to be a universal concern—truckers and their apparent disregard for the rules. My thoughts on the matter may surprise you.

I have been a cop for nineteen years. In all of that time I have honestly been in jeopardy of losing a battle, or even my life, only a few times. These were knockdown, drag-out brawls with rather large bad guys. Being large myself, it became clear that one of us was going to lose, and get hurt. Really badly. And in those few times it was looking as though it might be me. How's *that* for honesty!

On those few occasions I received help and, eventually, found my way home at the end of my shift. The help I received was completely unsolicited, for as I was wrestling I could not get to my radio. My help came not from a passing "4-wheeler" on the way to "Jellystone" with a minivan full of kids and potato chips, but from truck drivers. These men grabbed whatever they could—tire irons, baseball bats or sledgehammers—slammed on the brakes and came a-runnin'. So, if you want me to blanket all of these professionals with disfavor or derision, you came to the wrong place. They have my gratitude and respect. Now ... having said that ...

All of us have experienced a menace of a driver behind the wheel of forty tons of truck. Tailgating, speeding, swerving; and not caring for one moment what we think about it. Tired and dangerously unhealthy, with excessive hours, fatigue and sometimes under the influence of amphetamines, you must understand these are the very few of tens of thousands of skilled professionals who share your highways every day without incident. The good ones are some of the best and most careful drivers out there. Their livelihood depends on it.

None of us is without fault in our control over motor vehicles. Understanding this, keep in mind the average over-the-road driver crosses this country forty to fifty times each and every year, in all weather, at all times of the day and night. Could any of us drive that much and never goof?

My patrol car and badge, my ballistic vest, sidearm and trauma kit, all came to me in his truck—as did your pantry full of groceries, your aspirin and your baby's formula. Take it from me, most of these skilled professionals are just like you and me; with sound ethics and citizenship, intelligent and reasonable attitudes, compassion and understanding. And, as I have seen first hand ... unselfish courage.

Focus on them. My co-workers and I will deal with the others.

True Valor

Today, as I write this, it is Father's Day. Earlier, I called the finest man who ever lived and told him I was thinking of him. But it was he who beat me to the punch as he wished his son a Happy Father's Day. "Oh yeah," I said, "I guess I am a dad, too!"

This man—a retired police officer—once asked me why I would pursue the same profession, after watching the frustration and resignation he experienced as a cop during a time when police were anything but respected.

As a child growing up in the 1920's and 30's, he watched a sister die of tuberculosis, watched as a twelve-year-old as his father died of heart disease, and had a brother killed in a car crash. As a teenager, his family lost their farm in Ohio to the Depression and moved to Texas by covered wagon and horseback where they lived by sharecropping. Then, this same gentle man, enlisted in the Army to avoid high school history.

That was 1938. Three years later, the world was at war. He received his orders and carried a rifle into combat, where he was ordered to take the lives of as many enemy soldiers as he could. And with overwhelming fear, he did his duty. He was twenty. He was a child.

When the war was over he became a police officer and served with honor until his retirement some thirty years later. He had worked nights mostly, in the worst areas of Los Angeles and survived shootings, beatings, riots, campus demonstrations and the onset of a time where it seemed violent criminals had more rights than their victims.

Recently I told him I was very proud of him and his generation, because they truly had saved the world. I told him how proud he must be to know that a national memorial will soon be built to thank him and the millions of others who courageously served their country. His response completely deflated me but honestly did not surprise me.

I have heard him, and others like him, scoff or reject the accolades and tributes to their effort, saying, "We just did what we had to do. We stayed alive any way we could, and somehow managed to accept it." The many WWII veterans I have met, both here in Wyoming and across our country, have all seemed to share the desire to minimize their contribution to humanity. They simply came back to a very grateful country and resumed their lives, preferring to leave the horrid and bloody nightmare of what they had lived through back on the beaches, forests and jungles of other lands; far, far away.

In a police officer's career words of praise and admiration will be copious and heartfelt, and they will hear how brave and strong they are. They will have children and adults shaking their hands, or patting them on the shoulder, thanking them for the work they do. These citizens will use words like "courage" and "bravery" and "valor," and will wonder, sometimes aloud, how in the world we can do the job we do knowing the danger inherent to the work. And, they will seem humbled by our gallantry.

If I am honest, when I think of the men and women who served in that war—or any war for that matter—I acknowledge one, very simple truth:

Compared to them, my daring is trivial. And my heart is completely humble.

The Fudge Factor

"So ... just how fast can I go without being stopped?" asked a motorist I had just cited for doing eighty-nine miles per hour.

"Well," I told him with a smile, "that's classified. I could tell you, but then I'd have to kill you!"

He didn't get the joke and was not amused. This honest but heavy-footed motorist wanted a license to speed and I would not give him one. I went on to tell him I couldn't really answer, because to give a number would be permitting him to violate the law. My reasoning seemed of little consequence as he drove off mumbling incomprehensible expletives. He left me standing in a swirl of dust, next to where his car had been. I had destroyed a myth he had believed was as real as the car he was driving. I imagine his $200 fine didn't help much either.

Understanding the law is a good thing. You should have a clear and direct knowledge of all traffic laws, and under desirable circumstances you demonstrate this when you take your driving test. However, sometimes that knowledge can get a bit rusty. This can lead to tickets which can give you gas, acid reflux and sometimes, completely ruin your whole weekend.

The "fudge factor" is a myth at best in the mind of the violator and yes, sometimes, in the mind of the officer. Not in the law. Either you did it, or you did not. What each individual officer will use as a tolerance might be traffic density, weather or other factors. Not a certain speed or whether or not you call him names or approve of his mother. Under all but the most trying circumstances, good police officers do not allow emotion to influence decisions.

Most of us will, to a reasonable degree *at the time*, use the least invasive method of correction. Don't get all excited. You will be hammered for flagrant violations no matter how demure and apologetic you might be. What I'm talking about here are the minor violations. Those close to that imaginary "fudge factor." Each officer will have a different tolerance on different days in different weather for different reasons. See why we have to be vague? You just can't count on it.

The best bet is to just obey the law. Regarding speed, just give yourself time, set your cruise control at or under the limit and kick back. Having extra time allows you to drive leisurely and legally with consideration of the rest of the people using the highway. And it takes the pressure off so that when you think of fudge, it will simply be the sweet and creamy treat you love. Nothing else.

Menudo for Breakfast

It's been over twenty years since Candy Liktner founded MADD—Mothers Against Drunk Driving—and I'll bet you a cup of coffee her heart still aches very deeply into her soul every time she thinks of what her daughter might have become. All of the hugs and smiles they never shared. All of the magic a child brings a parent—ripped away—by an inconsiderate and selfish criminal who chose to drive after drinking too much.

In the years since, spanning some three decades now, endless public education, judicial education, legal education and police education has taken place—in a large way—conducted by the very people hurt the worst—the survivors. Those left behind to deal with the pain and loss this crime causes around the world. At their own behest, they founded these groups and created something incredibly effective from what must have certainly begun as the epitome of the "End of the World."

Today the problem persists. It is true many more are enlightened and aware of the problem, but unfortunately changes in the laws protecting us all from this danger have been painfully slow to come. Here in Wyoming, the penalty is still quite mild for violation of this law, but far better than it was when, for example, the drunken man who killed Trooper Pete Visser in 1981 received a total of six months in jail. Yes—*six months*.

When enforcement is lax or public awareness is low, the problem can easily get out of hand. Folks will always have parties and get-togethers full of good cheer and good booze. And if we're not real careful, some otherwise law abiding and solid good neighbors and friends might find themselves in jail or fighting for life, pinned in the burning wreckage of their car. Worse, someone's family—perhaps your own—out for a fun evening of shopping or visiting friends, quite innocent of anything wrong, could well be hurt very badly or killed. All under the guise of good cheer.

We in the law enforcement community stand ready with all of our skills and knowledge to protect you from as many of these people as possible. But, please understand that for every one of us there are many more of them. You must take certain steps yourself to avoid them.

Look for the telltale signs of drunk driving—driving too slow, straddling lanes, improper turning, failing to dim high beams and no signals. Avoid late night driving if possible and, of course, ALWAYS wear your safety belts for the ones that slip by! And call us if you see one. He may kill someone you know. Help us stop him.

Finally, to the guy who has the party, get this: You will be held directly liable in some courts for allowing excessive consumption and then allowing guests to drive home in bad shape should something happen. Avoid the headache and confiscate keys, serve food, provide a sober driver or two and a place to crash for the night.

And menudo for breakfast. Best cure for a hangover on Earth. Cheers!

Talking Speedometers

"But Officer...my speedometer said seventy-five," the otherwise honest motorist pleaded to no avail to the officer. Cutting short the dubious plea of innocence, the officer walked back to his patrol car, ran the license for status and scribbled out a pinch.

A speeding ticket. No matter whatcha call it, it means donating your money to the government—as if taxes aren't enough. And if it's one of too many, a suspended license and much higher insurance rates.

I never knew speedometers could talk until I got a badge. Suddenly I found out not only did they talk ... *they lied!* Never put too much trust in your speedometer. Off the showroom floor, even certified calibration police speedometers can be off one or two miles per hour! Yours can too! A tip: Ask a local peace officer to give you a speedometer check with RADAR, to give you the most accurate measurement available. Or use the old mile marker check.

If your speedometer is accurate, it should take you sixty seconds to go one mile at sixty miles per hour, while the same mile will take forty-nine seconds at seventy-five. Any less time means you are faster than indicated and you need to be aware of it! We would much rather give you this free advice now, than for you to find out by surprise and pay big bucks for a ticket! Remember that the law does not require speedometers; therefore, depending on your case, having an erroneous one may not help much in court.

We are fully aware the speed limit makes some people nuts. Remember that this law means many different things to so many different people, but the opinion of the police officer charged with enforcing it is truly a paradox. While obviously his is the most important one to you—it is irrelevant. He must enforce the law as written. What all agree on is this: The faster you go the higher the fine if you're busted. And the worse you will be hurt if you crash. It is just that simple.

While a speeding ticket is something most drivers will remember the rest of their lives, in a cop's world it is as mind-numbing as tying his shoes. On the scale of a cop's adrenaline addiction, it's about a one. Not that he doesn't take your emotions seriously but, really, do you remember every memo you've written, or customer you've checked out, or every coffee break conversation? Of course not. Do you actually remember tying your shoes yesterday?

In the end, oh yes, speedometers do talk. They tell you very clearly your approximate speed in a nice digital display with cute little lights and gauges, all to make your driving experience enjoyable and safe.

That little voice in there has another purpose as well. As you sit idly on the side of the road waiting patiently for the officer to complete the ticket, turn off your engine. If you listen real hard in the silence, you may hear a quiet little whisper, saying, ... "I told you so."

Jails, Jails, Jails!

One of the lousiest moments in life is the moment you realize something you like or love is not the perfect vision you had. Be it your spouse, your child, your car or your government, part of real life is understanding that Shangri-La just doesn't exist and we must do the best we can. Once this is realized the bitter lesson is making the best of it, and doing the right thing with difficult choices.

The United States, as starkly beautiful, spacious and diverse as it may be, is not perfect. Indeed, one of the reasons it is not is that it is inhabited by humans. Some 300 million of 'em. From time to time some of them break the rules of our society, and they need to be punished. As Americans, we have come up with humane incarceration as that punishment. Depriving freedom is our only way of spanking our naughty boys and girls. This is far too easy on them if you ask me and, so you see, that is why you don't let your cops do the punishing. The things we would come up with!

It has become painfully clear both as a peace officer and as a citizen who shares this space with you and pays his share of taxes, that we absolutely must pay up. Unless we want to let our law enforcement agencies swing in the wind for something completely out of their control yet completely their responsibility, we need to "cowboy up" and fork over the cash to build lots of new, warm and cozy places for our prisoners to have an enriching experience.

I say here and now to all who read my babbling that this matter—this costly and unpleasant expense—is absolutely 100% critical. It is proper and already years overdue. You as a society need more jails. No, not because it's cool to have new jails but because it's really, really cool not to have to give away our money to lawyers to fight the frivolous lawsuits filed by prisoners for inhumane treatment. The convicts are all too happy to cash in on our shortage of space! Wouldn't you rather use the money we are giving them to build a few roads, or bridges or libraries?

I am very proud to say that part of the reason our jails are constantly overflowing is the bang up job all in law enforcement are doing for you. Top notch professional peace officers; they bring them in day and night for everything from shoplifting to murder. From drunk driving to burglary. Crooks of all kinds. All of them are the people you have dictated you want removed from your streets and out of your life. And we are honored to go out there and get 'em for you. However, when we do, the plain and simple truth is we need to put them somewhere. That place is jail and, all joking and grumbling aside, in today's world a jail truly must measure up to court mandated comforts, features and security. Unfortunately, many existing slammers are woefully too small and built for another time—a past generation—both of criminal and of peace officer. Progress has its price and all of us must pay the bill.

My friends, it is time to "put your money where your mouth is" and vote for the funding to get these things built once and for all.

As unpleasant as it is to think of needing a multi-million dollar jail in your peaceful and prosperous community, imagine the ultimate price tag without it.

Filling in The Gaps

Several of my readers have shared thoughts with me about "wrong cops." Some, however, had official contact resulting in jail time so you can imagine their opinion. Discounting those, I am still left with many comments concerning virtue and moral fiber. Not only of those few who truly do go bad—but the others in the citizen's eye who are just as guilty of malfeasance because they do not report or speak out against the cops they "know" are bad.

First understand something. Every good cop will agree with those who demand removal from office when sworn police officers breach their word to you and betray the badge. Having said that, you must understand the foundation of training good police officers—the 99% you *can* trust—receive initially and throughout their careers. Much of it is about honest reporting of what they *know* to be true. Not what they *think* to be true, or what they *want* to be true.

Police officers are bound by sworn oath and professional ethics not to summarize, condense, conceal, color or enhance the facts. They are to report and act expressly and exclusively on factual truths—

not innuendo or suspicion alone. While it is arguable that indeed over time some of my brethren have perhaps "filled in the gaps" in reporting (as a well-known Wyoming lawyer puts it), I submit once again that this is true only with a very, very few. Unfortunately, when you recruit humans it happens.

I personally have struggled with myself when I have remembered a crucial fact or observation which I may have overlooked. And as I write my report, I know that because I have failed here a very guilty person is going to walk. Because of my human imperfection, a crucial piece of evidence will not be allowed—one that everybody in the courtroom *knows* would prove the guy was guilty. Without it he walks. In our system it is an extremely painstaking process to deprive freedom. It should be. So he walks. Can you see the temptation to save face and … "fill in the gaps?"

Just "hearing about" a bad cop is something filed away in the mind and perhaps reported to a supervisor, but in and of itself cannot be acted upon. You can't "fill in the gaps" here either. Not only would it be libelous if unfounded, but we may unjustly and unethically remove an honorable and brave man or woman from a profession which demands integrity and morality above reproach. You see, once accused of anything less, a police officer is forever, from that day on, branded an outcast from the fraternity. Like the man accused of rape or child abuse but later exonerated, he is scarred and can never again fit into the fold without a small cloud of suspicion always there no matter how unfounded the charges might have been.

In the world of law enforcement, trust takes on a completely new meaning. I don't know what you do for a living, but at my office the guy "watching my back" really is. And I trust him not just with my Day Planner and Rolodex, but with my very life. The trust between our special fraternity goes to the bone and if ever soiled it is gone forever.

Perhaps when you understand this, you can understand the seemingly dilatory process we use in weeding our little garden. Never to protect a "wrong cop," but rather to maintain the trust of the virtuous who offer their honesty and their life to you.

Be Careful

Since cops are reluctant to expose (a hazard of the job) emotions, two simple words have become our best gesture of fraternity and truly heartwarming when offered by a citizen or neighbor. A simple wish to do what we must do to make it home.

If you live 100 years, you will never hear two cops (at least two male cops) say they "love" each other, all warm and fuzzy with eye contact and everything! It's not gonna happen folks. Not a chance. So, the expression "be careful" becomes a non "touchie-feelie" and thereby completely cool and non-threatening way for cops to say, "Hey, I care about you very much."

When offered from concerned citizens who have become aware of the dangers faced by their police, this expression is reassuring and warmly received. We often don't give the public enough credit for understanding our fears, or for their prayers or genuinely good wishes. In many communities around the country there is a long-held practice among churches to divvy up the names of all of the peace officers in the area and each week ask the members to offer prayers for them—by *name*! I was completely stunned the first time a friend walked up to me and said, "Hey, Big Jim! Your name came up last Sunday! We prayed for you! Were your ears ringing?" I have never forgotten that. It is good in this business to have Divine backup!

There are many unseen and subtle tactics we use out there to ensure our safety, and any cop on the job for a few months soon comes to understand them. The obvious things are the ballistic armor we wear and weapons we carry. However, day to day the art of "being careful" is as simple as a verbal challenge or as subtle as a quick glance you don't even see. Have you ever noticed when speaking to police officers on the street they rarely look at you; but instead look you and everyone else up and down to size things up?

Have you ever noticed we watch your hands more than your face? Have you ever noticed how we stand; keeping a distance and wide stance? Have you ever offered a handshake to one of us, only to have it ignored?

These actions are not because of cheesy manners. Your police are aware it sometimes looks like we are about as stiff as a refrigerator box, but please understand everything we do is *deliberate*. These and the hundreds of other tactics we keep under wraps (super-secret agent stuff) have origins and reasons you may not know or understand, but I hope you appreciate. Generations of cops taken from their families have taught us these lessons. Gifts left to us to make our job just a little safer. These sacrifices cannot be made in vain.

As recent events have shown, please understand any person you see with a badge, regardless of the uniform, has dedicated their life to bringing about the very essence of what this humanity is—human decency and kindness. In this quest there is always danger.

Next time you see a man or woman in uniform close at hand, offer a simple admonishment to "be careful." It truly is the most supportive and loving message you can give. For you've told a cop, "Hey, I care about you very much."

Doing Winter

One thing is for sure, winter isn't for amateurs. In the big city, to be caught out there in the farthest reaches of the realm with no forethought will result merely in an inconvenient side trip to the closest convenience store. Here in "God's Country", it can mean life and death. It is that serious. Believe it.

Mrs. Geeting and other "native" friends will say, "Surviving winter is easy! What's the big deal? Just stock up, stay home and wait until it's safe to go. Jeesh...next question?"

In Wyoming for example, if your life requires travel, "doing winter" is much, much more than just turning up the defroster, putting on your thermals and sipping a cup of hot cocoa while you drive. If you spend any time on the road, it's putting water dispersant additive in your gas tank, snow and mud tires all around, sandbags in your trunk and tossing in some chains, water, blankets, canned foods and nuts, gloves, fuzzy hats, boots, flashlights, candles, books and even a few logs and fire starter pellets. An *inflated* spare tire with *a jack that works* is smart, not to mention a driver who knows how to use them! If you don't know how (and it would amaze you how many don't), *learn*. It could save your life. Flats happen even in snowstorms and the less time you have to spend in that driving, sub-zero wind reading the instructions while other drivers cannot see you, the quicker you'll be fixed and getting home.

Becoming disoriented and then stranded out on some dirt road in the height of a blizzard is something many lifelong Wyoming residents have done, thinking they were on the paved highway. One time I walked up to the window of a guy who was spinning his tires in a blizzard. I knocked on his window and about gave him a heart attack! I motioned him to roll down his window and he looked down at my feet. He thought he was moving along on US191 about twenty mph or so according to his speedometer. He had unknowingly driven into the shoulder and was high-centered spinning his tires! While I have laughed more than once about this, I scared the berjeebers out of this guy. Disorientation like this is much more common than you might think.

Commonly, we make three big mistakes in bad weather. Our first is when we become impatient and drive off from home when waiting an hour or even a day wouldn't have hurt too badly or messed up our plans beyond repair. The second is when we get stuck or stranded out there, then start out on foot to look for help. Hypothermia is absolutely deadly, and those lights you see out there in the distance may be only a mile away, but in even mildly cold weather one mile might as well be ten. Stay with the warmth and visibility of your car. Fight the urge to try for it, and stay put! Let *us* find *you*.

Finally, the third mistake is communication, or lack of it. If you haven't yet discovered the safety and convenience of a cell phone, get one. This is the single best safety device yet for traveling. Get one!

If you don't have to go out there, count your blessings. Break out your favorite book and those jammies you got for Christmas and send out a kind thought or two to those of us who do.

Lost Victims

Others more intellectually gifted than I have discussed the stress associated with police work, and I do not pretend to be an expert on the physiological effects and chemical reactions occurring in the body when stress builds. I do know there are unique factors that complicate the matter in police officers. Tragically, this leads to a suicide rate two to three times greater than the general public. For these lost victims, relief comes only in the finality of self-destruction. In memory of one such friend, I offer this:

First, understand that there is no way to measure the effect of the physical, visual and emotional assault a police officer is subjected to with each shift. People at their worst. Death and bloody gore, and intentional infliction of injury and pain. And despair in the eyes of children who look up and pray you are their savior—there to fix their alcoholic or abusive caregiver. Other stressors, like being shot at, beat up, cut up or run over in a traffic crash, obviously add to the damage.

How many prowlers have you had to hunt down in the blackness of 3:00 AM in some backyard, knowing you'll never see the attack coming? How many humans, ground into a pulp in a high speed traffic crash, have you had to somehow lift into a body bag as the liquefied mess spills all about? Things like this happen routinely for a police officer, and the emotional toll is very expensive. The mental scars these scenes etch into a cop's brain are there forever, haunting with the smells, sounds and screams replayed each time the memory is nudged from its resting place.

And rather than release this tension as most folks can do by openly seeking the professional help of a therapist or psychologist, the police officer's mentality dictates they must remain steadfast and strong, while their heart is breaking or they are experiencing depression. For in this profession, one's peers see it as a sign of weakness to be troubled enough to seek help.

The classic warning signs of a breakdown or contemplated suicide won't always show on a police officer. Remember, the police officer is an expert—both from their training and from years of swallowing their hurting heart—in suppressing their feelings of infuriating anger, hopelessness, sadness and physical pain. Police officers are a living example of "walking off" minor pain—both physical and mental. Unlike a sore muscle, mental pain remains unless compassionately extracted. Friends, brother and sister cops, and family should encourage a loved police officer experiencing post-traumatic stress to be honest enough to say "I NEED HELP" out loud! And, they must be strong when that police officer rejects the suggestion. I assure you, he or she will.

I pray that my bothers and sisters out there will understand that seeking help is not weakness. It is strength and valor of the finest kind. It is a statement that although hurting, we want more than anything else to go on. To fight. To live. To serve humanity for years to come.

With the compassion of the public, the people who love us or serve with us, we can.

Radar Love

The one tool police use which has caused the most controversy, court time, arguments on the side of the road, complete frustration and increased insurance rates has been traffic radar. So many misunderstandings and ill-conceived beliefs exist about it; and really, it is a simple and proven device accepted as accurate *provided* it is used correctly.

RADAR is not a real word—it's an acronym. It stands for **RA**dio **D**irection **A**nd **R**anging. It was developed for use in World War II to locate enemy aircraft and to help aviators guide themselves to targets or back home. Radar works because of some scientist named Doppler. I couldn't tell you his first name but I'll betcha he was pretty smart.

Anyway, this Doppler dude came up with and proved a scientific principle—the Doppler Principle—that says as objects move closer or farther away, the sound waves they make change frequency in direct relation to that movement because they are compressed or stretched. Don't believe me?

Stand (at a safe distance, please) next to a highway. As cars approach the sound will raise in pitch as the distance "compresses" or closes toward you. Then, as it passes, that same pitch will drop as the sound waves stretch or decrease in frequency. A better example is a jet taking off or a train blowing its air horn as it passes by the crossing you are stopped at.

Meanwhile, back at the lab, a radio signal of a known frequency was transmitted out, and it actually bounced off the objects in its path and returned to the radio receiver; altered to a different frequency. The difference became known as the Doppler Frequency. That frequency is converted by the radar computing unit into a range away or an altitude. Or, in our case, a speed.

It worked! Scientifically, it was proven there was nothing faster or more accurate. The signal traveled at the speed of light and was out there and back in a few nanoseconds. But then the human factor came in.

Traffic radar is operated by human beings highly trained but not infallible. A Wyoming state trooper, for example, receives a full week of classroom and practical training before ever being issued a radar unit. Then with a training officer, competency must be proven in the field. But like any other human, the officer can goof. While I will not try to defend or explain individual problems, I will say they exist.

I encourage you now, as I have encouraged all I ever cited, to stand up for yourself in court if you truly and honestly *know* you did not violate the speed limit. You might still lose, but you just might *win*! As a professional law enforcement officer I understand my humanity and imperfection. While trying to do my duty without flaws or seams, sometimes they do show. And when they do it is pointed out clearly by the person in the robe.

By the way, I have never clocked a tree doing ninety-five. If I ever do, I think a warning will suffice.

Stuff

One of the coolest things about being a cop is that you get *stuff*. Lots and lots of cool *stuff*. You get to wear sparkling golden or silver trinkets and decorations. If you ask children, one of the coolest things is the "Bat Belt," upon which are hung all of our primary tools and gadgets. A different kind of "tool belt" guy.

Made of squeaky polished leather sometimes stitched plain and sometimes in a basketweave design, it carries our primary tools should we need them. First, and certainly the most ominous, is our gun. Some hold lots of bullets, some only six. All are of large caliber, and in the possession of a police officer, quite deadly though safely secured. Always there to protect you or us if needed, but left alone unless there is no other option. While there isn't one of us who would do this job without one, we all pray it will never be fired in combat—right up to the day we pass it on to a younger brave soul. And then may *he* never need it.

Also hangin' around are less threatening tools such as handcuffs, pepper spray and a baton. These too are left right there unless some grumpy soul wants to ruin our day or mess up yours. These items (all of them) require weeks of extensive training in both the legal and tactical aspects, and are used only when verbal skill and hand-to-hand compliance techniques will not persuade a person to stop whatever lousy, mean thing they are doing. When this happens we can usually convince them in very short order.

You get a fast car with lots of flashing lights, a P.A. system and two different radios with dozens of different channels so we can talk to just about anyone in the world. The modern day police car carries other tools as well. Like gloves. Gloves are big with cops. Usually four different pair. One pair for when it is -5 degrees and windy, and another for digging through the jagged and sharp metal of a crash. A third pair for searching bad guys who might have sharp goodies purposely concealed to cut our hands and, finally, another set for handling hurt and bloody people. There are many icky diseases out there which live in human blood. We do NOT want to take one home.

A trauma kit, flares, traffic cones, signs, shovels, fire extinguishers, long-range weapons, ropes, tow straps, measuring wheels, tapes and flashlights. But wait! There's more!

Any number of official forms and paperwork, gas masks, speed measuring instruments, road spikes, extra ammunition, personal breath testers (no, not for halitosis—for testing breath alcohol) and blankets. Some carry truck scales, hazardous materials identification kits, hard hats, tactical gear, riot helmets, special weapons, supplies and extra jackets. Most carry something else as well …

It might be a small "Hot Wheels" police car. Maybe an anniversary card or love letter. Or a child's soft animal or blanket. A "Happy Birthday" card or a pretty marble. Perhaps a photograph or lock of hair, or a Mother's Day gift. A baseball card or masterpiece crayon colored drawing of a ladybug. A doll or a G.I Joe. A plastic Easter Egg with a child's surprise inside, or perhaps, a test paper with a great big A+! A neat rock or a pretty and special pencil. A miniature teacup, or "Easy Bake" cookies.

This is the coolest "stuff" of all.

Ice Ain't Nice

Ice is a true paradox. Sometimes your finest friend like when you sprain your ankle and need to reduce swelling. Or, when it cools your cooler full of beverages on a fishing trip. On the other hand, ice can kill you. Some friend.

On the roadway ice is worthy of your utmost attention and respect. When your tires are rubbing against dry pavement, they are quite sticky and that's what grabs the road; especially on curves. That's a good thing.

Then along comes a patch of ice. This sticky quality goes instantly to zero and the pavement becomes like Teflon. Then you say aloud whatever your favorite word is when you know you're in trouble. Suddenly there is an eerie silence, where just a moment ago there was tire rumble. *That* is a *bad* thing. A *very* bad thing.

Many things will affect your outcome when driving on ice. Wind, vehicle weight and distribution, chains or studs, wheelbase and road grade. But friends, if you lose traction on frozen water, there is only one thing in this world that will make the difference of whether you live and escape injury, or get really banged up, or perhaps worse. Your speed.

Excessive speed on ice is like repairing a toaster while it's plugged in. Disaster is inevitable. It's nothing personal, but ice at that instant in time is absolutely unforgiving, cold-blooded, ruthless and mean. One wrong bump or gust; perhaps a sudden control change and just like that you are sliding—completely out of control. Maybe into a guardrail destroying your car. Conceivably into the median sideways, where you may roll over and if not wearing your seat belts be ejected and crushed. Perhaps off the edge of a mountain road, unseen and unheard! Or one of my personal nightmares, across the median and head-on into oncoming traffic. Anyway . . .

The trick to driving on ice is not to unless absolutely necessary. It will never be completely safe if you do have to travel, but it can be done. If you find you will be traveling on ice, quadruple your travel time and slow down; *way down!* If you're suddenly surprised and have indeed uttered that special word you use, no need to panic—just use the "off" button on your cruise control or *gradually* ease off the gas pedal—slowly, slowing down. *DO NOT TOUCH THE BRAKES! DO NOT MAKE SUDDEN STEERING MOVEMENTS!* Feel free to utter that favorite word. Often and loud!

If you are originally from a place where ice was unheard of you have company. Me for instance. I'm a former "California dude" and I was just like you (amazed and actually frightened) by the horror stories about devastation and carnage on icy roads. *Huh? Icy roads?* Like dude, you can get ice? On the *road?* The stories are true. Listen to long-time residents of any winter wonderland and heed their advice.

Best advice on icy days? Stay home and read a good book. Perhaps this one!

On Being Human

Every peacemaker I know was first an infant with stinky diapers, new teeth and needing to be burped. Then time and circumstances step in, molding a grownup who, for a variety of reasons ends up holding a sacred office and the power of life and death on their hip. He or she is bestowed a badge of honor and depending on which agency they end up with, any one of a variety of costumes. All designed to identify them as one of the good guys and somehow a cut above.

There are tall ones and short ones, men and women, old whiskers and kids with peach fuzz. All colors, religions and even all political parties. A wondrous variety indeed. All human, all different.

Woodworkers and musicians … writers and actors … pilots and race car drivers. Rock climbers and chess players … computer geeks and grease monkeys. All cops. All good neighbors. All very brave. But human, and as such, flawed.

Did you ever see a police car driving too fast or "ooze" through a stop sign? Or forget to signal a lane change? Sure you have. Ever hear one of us cuss in public or slip on the ice, fall and get up with that cat-like "I meant to do that" look on a red face? You know you have. What did you see there? Did you see disgraceful conduct or humanity? Were you ashamed or did you understand?

While your local police officers, sheriff's deputies or state troopers and agents are trained and equipped to handle just about any trouble life or nature sends to our county, all of us have a flaw in our character and a weakness. It is our membership in the family of man, complete with all that entails. We can sometimes have bad breath or bad attitudes; impatience or intolerance. Or just like you, we can just have had a bad day.

In those moments; those brief seconds where we reveal the down side, our hope is that nobody saw nothin' and we go on. On to patrol your back alleys at 3:00 AM for prowlers. To calm your neighborhood or domestic disputes. To protect your children from evil. To remove the dangers all around you. And as we do this—as we have do deal with that part of humanity—our hope is that you clearly understand ours.

Trust

Recently a reader sent me an email questioning a law requiring motorists to merge away from emergency vehicles when encountering one of us stopped on the side of the road. This same law requires slowing to twenty mph under the speed limit on two-lane highways when passing a stopped emergency vehicle. While the reader is an outspoken supporter of law enforcement, albeit with a justified demand of respectful treatment of citizens, he wondered if an ill-motivated police officer could abuse his authority, as the law is open to subjective judgment in its enforcement. The answer was yes—as it is for many Uniform Traffic Code statutes.

Punative enforcement or a warning for minor violations is entirely within the authority and "call" of the officer on the street. Consider this. If we as a society trust the police officer with the power of life and death literally and instantly within immediate reach, is it a stretch to trust that same officer's sense of fair play and just application of the law? I think so. I know so.

Obviously my opinion here is tainted and entirely biased. But it is not blind. As I have written many times, good cops acknowledge and accept the infallible and inescapable flaw of all police officers—their humanity. It is true over the 225 years of American law enforcement that the human pool of candidates has provided the occasional bad seed. But, taken as a whole profession, my brothers and sisters, no matter the agency, are men and women whose judgment, leadership and sense of fairness you *can* trust. I do every day. I trust them not only with the law, but also with my life. And as recent events have proven, their courage is immeasurable. Their devotion complete.

Accepting the truth that all humanity is less than perfect will allow you to see the height of love and compassion possessed by these people you pay to protect you. You will see as I have that near the top of many others in various callings in your community will be your law enforcement family. If you could see the individual histories of each officer—each prowler she caught; each drunk driver he nabbed and each violent criminal deterred from committing some bloody crime against you—you would never again question their valor or integrity. If you could see the hours of study, the lifetime of abstinence from vice, and a character free of common acceptance of what some call "minor" criminal behavior, you would never again question their character.

And, if you could know the hundreds upon hundreds of minor infractions and boo-boos committed by otherwise honest and good drivers which are consciously overlooked and allowed to go undetected every day by all police officers because their judgment was that the mistake you made was just that, you would understand. And you would never again question the motives of any officer who does stop you to enforce the law.

Trust me on this one.

Chapter Five
End of Watch

A Complete Community

Community support, or lack of it, is sometimes the best reflection of the success of a law enforcement agency. A history of abuse, excessive force, or corruption paint a dubious portrait of every officer and makes those they need to contact step back from them or hold back crucial information they may have otherwise offered. This is a shameful waste—as most officers I have known have been the zenith of good and honor.

Conversely, when the agency and individual officers are trusted, as is thankfully the case in most Wyoming communities, information and vocal support are readily given and immediately evident. Citizens of communities who trust their police will sometimes show this by simple demonstrations of esteem. A nod, a smile, or the familiar "Wyoming Wave;" that thing we do in Wyoming where the fingers are lifted from the steering wheel as we pass by a neighbor. Or a friend, like a local officer in a patrol car. At other times these demonstrations are more intense and incredibly meaningful.

A few years ago we buried a Wyoming state trooper killed in the line of duty. He was my friend and an honorable citizen, with respect for his community and country. His funeral was conducted with full police honors. The procession of police cars from all over the state and region, totaling over 100, was awe-inspiring. Part of the route brought us through downtown Douglas, one of the small communities so plentiful in our state. The historic buildings, old store fronts and sidewalks that welcome visitors to that community were clean and well-kept. On the sidewalk in front of a barbershop, a man was walking with his preschool-aged son. Both wore matching John Deere ball caps. They walked hand in hand, discussing the things discussed between a man and his boy. Then they saw us coming.

At first I saw the boy point; an expression on his face of curious wonder at all the bright, shining police cars with red and blue lights flashing. Then I saw his father kneel down next to him. He was explaining what they were witnessing—police officers paying respect to a fallen comrade. Finally, as I drove past them I was humbled, flattered and filled with gratitude as I witnessed something I had never seen.

The man and then his boy, who had obviously been instructed by his father, stood erect and still, removed their ball caps and held them over their hearts. They stood motionless in that way, the look of wonder never leaving the little boy's face.

Later, during the service when the American flag was folded and presented to the trooper's wife, I glanced across the street, trying to avoid this heartbreaking sight. When I did I saw an enormous crowd of citizens. Not one a police officer.

As the entire detail of peace officers snapped to a salute at the order of "Present Arms," the mournful, final message of "Taps" blared out, played by an unseen bugler. Standing in rigid salute I again looked across the street and saw men in suits, women in dresses and bikers wearing leathers. There were even a few grocery clerks and meat cutters standing there in their dirty aprons. Fighting the swelling pain in my throat, I saw a complete community sharing our pain. Many cried aloud. Others, like that little boy and his daddy, placed hands over their hearts.

This was a complete community, who felt this loss as deeply as we did. I was reminded once again why I do this.

For them.

May 15—Police Memorial Day

You want some truth? Some cops in this country will die on the job. Usually one every other day or so. In 2001, due to September 11, that number was much higher. May 15th is our day to honor them. God bless them all.

Every May 15 is National Law Enforcement Memorial Day. On October 1, 1962, authorized by a joint resolution of the United States Congress, President Kennedy made that proclamation and the entire week of May 15 is now National Police Week.

Did you know your police have a National Memorial? It's in Washington, D.C., at Judicial Square, just down the street from the Ford Theater, FBI Headquarters and the Naval Memorial. This is law enforcement's most sacred ground.

With each Memorial Service I have attended, conducted by the President of the United States, I have stood in silent reverence as the names of the officers killed on the job in the previous year were read aloud. I have seen gifts left at the memorial near the names of loved ones—teddy bears, favorite candy, departmental patches and flowers. And letters.

Children like to leave letters (sometimes private and sealed), the envelope of which simply scribbled in crayon with, "DADDY" or "MOMMY." It is devastating just to see them.

At one service a little boy of six or seven dressed in a snappy suit ran up and down a long line of us. We were all in different uniforms—standing there in silent attention—having saluted at the command of "Present Arms!" The boy ran and ran and ran, seemingly looking for someone. As the distant buglers then played the sad lament of "Echo Taps", I was thankful I was wearing sunglasses. I knew who he was looking for.

Finally, he ran back to his mother sitting close by in the huge crowd and through his tears exclaimed, "Mommy, maybe one is Daddy! Maybe Daddy's here!" She pulled him to her lap. Her whispered explaination deeply reminded him again of the truth that had some time back ended his boyhood. Instantly.

Later I saw him again at "The Wall." Standing next to his mom he stood facing his dad's name on the granite facade. The boy let go of his mother's hand and walked up to the wall. He kneeled down and reached out, placing something near a name. It was none of my business, but I had to know. After they had gone, I walked over to where they had been.

Taped to the wall were two unused box seat tickets to a baseball game the year before between the Yankees and the Dodgers. A note—this one purposely left open and written for him by his mom—read simply, "Dear Daddy, can we go to another game? We missed this one. Is there baseball in heaven? I love you. Say Hi to God! Love, Your Son, Arnold." That night I called home from my hotel and heard the lovely sound of my wife's voice. I shared this day with her and told her how much it hurt.

A few days later I returned to Wyoming and held a world-class-pile-on wrestling match with my own two sons—then, ages five and seven. Normally, Mrs. Geeting doesn't go for such roughhousing.

On that day she never said a word.

Retirement—The Big Payoff

Something that comes up in conversations with regular people is a cop's retirement—the one big perk we have. In exchange for offering up our lives to protect our people, and doing so nights, graveyards and holidays for twenty to thirty years missing school and family events and a less then lucrative paycheck, we are allowed to retire at an age some find a bit young. It is society's way of saying, you take care of us for awhile, and we'll take care of you. Good trade!

In many systems, an officer who starts at twenty-one years old can draw 50% pay at forty-one. 75% at fifty-one. Not a bad deal. Of course this is still far too young to stop working, and the retired cop is free to pursue a new career—a real job where something useful is produced and nobody tries to kill you. And, of course, all the while drawing that check from their prior life as a cop! The payoff. For risking death, mayhem and pain.

The reasoning for this type of retirement is the same as the military—in fact it is modeled after it. The work like that of a soldier is a young man's game. It is physically, emotionally and mentally taxing. It demands youth, physical strength and good health.

Two decades of living in a fishbowl and working in constant danger, high caution and always under many critical eyes builds a stress level twice that of regular people. Virtually all modern psychologists—not just those specializing in police psychology—agree. The job of a cop literally beats the body down. And come on. At sixty-four perhaps blessed with grandkids, would you really want to be wrestling for your life with some twenty-five-year-old felon all alone out on some lonely highway? Me neither!

Some of us retire from one agency just to move on to another. Some run for political office—especially the office of County Sheriff—because the need to serve just will not subside. There are some who go to the other extreme.

My dad turned in his badge and promptly came home, took off his watch and creamed it with a five-pound sledgehammer. He had lived by the clock for too long and he never has since. He was a cop for thirty years.

I was once attending a meeting of the Wyoming Highway Patrol Association—our fraternal group. In walks this scuzbag and sits down at our meeting table! Instinctively, I stepped away, unsure what to do. Completely befuddled, I wanted to frisk him and run a check on him for wants and warrants! With a beard down to there and hair down to here, wearing multiple gold chains and a twelve-inch Bowie knife on his belt, I thought I'd met a real Wyoming mountain man. I hadn't. I had met a retired division commander of the WHP, and one who had served with distinct honor.

The man had just had enough of haircuts, shaving and conforming to a conservative look, and truly had left the profession behind. God bless him. A lifetime member of our association, he just stopped by to be with his friends.

Someday soon my turn will come to grow my hair, throw out my razor and smash my Timex. When that day comes it will be with a mixture of elation and indeed some sadness. I will have worked my last shift protecting the lives and families of others.

And as I sleep in my home at night, every night, another will be out there protecting mine. Good trade.

About the Author

Jim Geeting is a working Wyoming State Trooper. He has been serving in Wyoming law enforcement since 1982, with service on the Wyoming Highway Patrol and Evanston Police Department. He has been decorated with the Distinguished Service Medal for successful criminal negotiations, and the Purple Heart for injuries on the job. He has received two coveted "Colonel's Commendations" from two different WHP Administrators, and he appeared as himself in a hair-raising episode of "The Real Stories of the Highway Patrol" television series, reenacting one of his negotiations with an armed felon.

Jim is certified as an Academy Instructor for officer survival and traffic stops, and as a Field Training Officer. He served for eight years on the Wyoming Highway Patrol Special Services Squad (reactionary team), and served for four years as president of the Wyoming Highway Patrol Association.

A writer since the third grade, he is the editor of the *Wyoming State Trooper,* the WHP fraternal magazine. For the last few years he has been writing his column, *The Badge,* twice a month in the *Rock Springs Daily Rocket Miner* and monthly in Wyoming's largest newspapers—the *Casper Star Tribune* and the *Cheyenne Tribune Eagle.*

Over his career Jim became frustrated with the lofty arrogance a few in his profession seemed to display, and he vowed to offer a word or two from one of the vast majority—the regular men and women who do police work as a profession, not as a lifestyle.

He speaks to the reader not as a cop who writes, but as the husband of a schoolteacher, the father of two teenaged sons and a neighbor who happens to be a cop. He discusses in a friendly, plain-spoken way the dynamics and human interactions police officers live with on a daily basis—the special relationship between cops and kids, cops and other cops, cops and criminals, and the unique challenges peace officers face in maintaining a normal family life.

He has received the prestigious Pace Maker Award from the Wyoming Press Association, and still writes the column today.

Printed in the United States
1001500003B